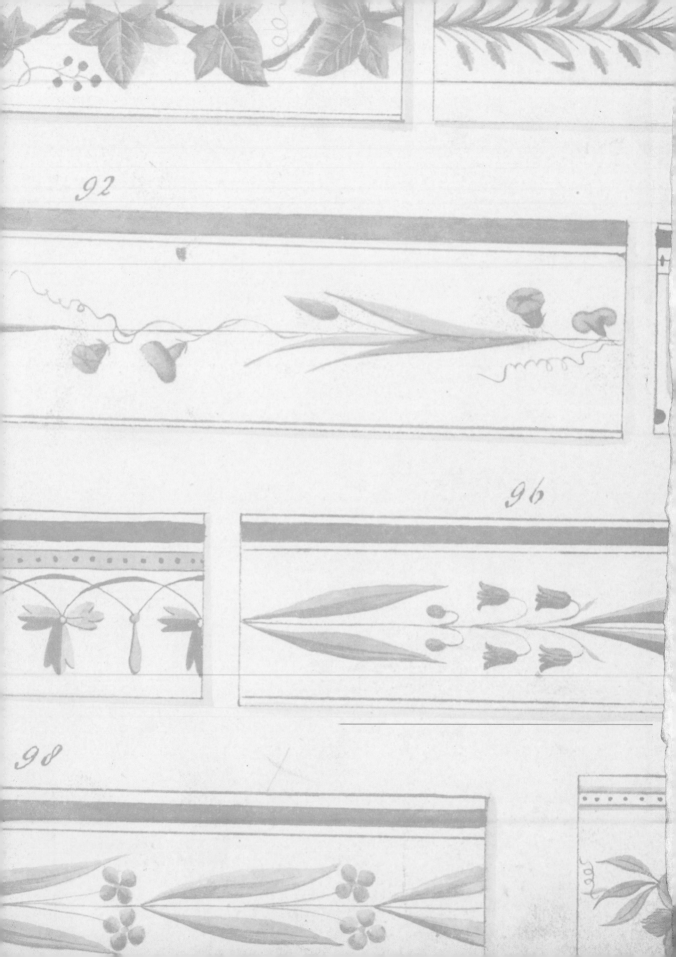

92

96

98

AT HOME WITH WEDGWOOD

TRICIA FOLEY

TEXT BY CATHERINE CALVERT   PHOTOGRAPHS BY JEFF McNAMARA

CLARKSON POTTER PUBLISHERS | NEW YORK

AT HOME WITH
WEDGWOOD

THE ART OF THE TABLE

Published in the United States by
Clarkson Potter/Publishers, an imprint of the
Crown Publishing Group, a division of
Random House, Inc., New York.
www.crownpublishing.com
www.clarksonpotter.com

CLARKSON POTTER is a trademark and POTTER with
colophon is a registered trademark of Random House, Inc.

Library of Congress Cataloging-in-Publication Data
is available upon request.

ISBN 978-0-307-45184-2

Printed in China

Design by Marysarah Quinn

10 9 8 7 6 5 4 3 2 1

FIRST EDITION

All photos by Jeff McNamara, except for the following:

Quentin Bacon: pages 2, 3, 4, 5, 28, 29, 110, 111, 153, 162, 164, 165
Christoph Kircherer: pages 94, 96, 97
Mikkel Vang: pages 140, 141
By courtesy of the Wedgwood Museum Trust, Barlaston, Staffordshire: pages 12, 15, 17, 19, 20, 22, 26 (portraits of
Lady Templetown, Eric Ravilious, Susie Cooper, and Emile Lessore), 27 (portraits of John Flaxman, Josiah Wedgwood,
and Keith Murray) and the endpaper art

To the spirit of
Josiah Wedgwood

CONTENTS

DESIGNED FOR TODAY 111

TIMELESS TRADITIONS 139

FOREWORD

For almost thirty years, I have traveled around the world meeting people who love Wedgwood. It thrills me to see the Wedgwood enthusiasts who come to see what's new or share stories of the Wedgwood they own. People have a real connection to the company through their prized pieces. Even young people, especially those who are about to get married, are intent on learning all they can about Wedgwood, and I always tell them that its quality will last for their lifetime and make each meal special.

As a small boy, I was drawn to the excitement of the factory, where I watched the china move from lump of clay to finely painted plate. I became part of the process as a teenager: In the summertime I would work at mastering the skills of the potter, which were taught to me by the craftspeople. Soon I was convinced that I wanted to work for Wedgwood. In 1980 I became an "International Ambassador" for the company, and today I travel all around the world to represent Wedgwood in various roles. I continue to be charmed by all I've seen and the people I've met.

The Wedgwood family motto is *Obstantia Discindo:* "I overcome all obstacles." As a member of the board of directors, I have seen that determination in action as I watch the company continue to innovate as well as preserve the prime values that have been sustained for two and a half centuries: quality, invention, a distinctive style, and a concern for our customers.

These were the very values Josiah Wedgwood himself served, and they inspired him to create one of the very first internationally successful companies. As you read the history and stories in Tricia Foley's wonderful book, you will come to share the passion I feel about Wedgwood's tremendous heritage and timeless designs.

—Lord Wedgwood

INTRODUCTION

I arrived at Wedgwood in 1987 to work for a company with a long and interesting history of quality. I knew that Wedgwood had always produced beautiful objects with impeccable craftsmanship and design.

One afternoon, in the midst of counting inventory with Earl Buckman at his Dallas shop, Ivy House, I caught a glimpse of an exquisite object: a classic midnight blue and white jasper jug with translucent dancing ladies on it—sheer bliss! The piece went home with me, beginning a lifetime collection of vintage Wedgwood.

Earl talked about Josiah Wedgwood, the company's founder, who had created this object I found so immediately charming. I listened intently as Earl told me how a boy in northern England, driven by curiosity and new ideas, became a creative genius who started a global business. I read the company's history and discovered riches hidden in its archives. I saw beautiful examples of chinaware he'd designed, and his experiment books and letters told me more about his unquenchable drive, as well as his humor. In time, I was enthralled by more than the china: Josiah Wedgwood himself completely won me over. His vision amazed me. He was so dedicated to making quality pottery and china that he was both an inventor and a designer. He created his successful life from bare beginnings, maintaining a lifelong commitment to social justice. And, as someone who has worked in retailing her whole life, I was thoroughly impressed by what a clever marketer he was! He both understood what people needed and created new ideas of style and luxury for them. He made Wedgwood an international name brand in a period when many potters never thought beyond their own village.

Now that I am CEO of Wedgwood and Royal Doulton, I find myself remembering his lessons: to look for creative ideas. To know what the customers need—and to lead fashion into the future. To be part of everyone's everyday life, and at the same time to create unique and precious wares. At Wedgwood we strive to replicate Josiah's gift for designs so perfect that most have lasted for two hundred fifty years. Innovation, perseverance, and artistry: All of Wedgwood works with these values, Josiah Wedgwood's own, before us.

—MOIRA GAVIN, CEO, WEDGWOOD

THE STORY OF
WEDGWOOD

Sytch Brook

To the Bi...

Scale 100 yards to the inch

Based on a plan by Enoch Wood

Hill Meadow

Oxley Croft

Oldfield

The Sytch

Thos. Shaw

Moses Marsh

Taylor's Hill

The Hill

The Hill

Big Hill

ttle
s spot
I was 150 yds. west

Little

The HILL

Wm. Follows

Fra. Rogers

Clark Mulkin

Jno. Mitchell   Wm. Horden

Chell   John Simpson

Wm. Stevenson

Josiah Simpson

Mme. Egerton

Thos. Bennet

Thos. Ward
Thos. Read

J. & T. Moore
Eph. Booth
Jno. Moore
Ric. Steele
Mr. Wm. Stevenson

Potworks   Taylors

Overhouse

John Wood (exiseman)
Xtopher Owen

The Jenkins

Mr. Thos. Mitchell   John Mitchell

Hill Top   Bridget Shaw

Ho.

Sarah Cartlich
Ranle Buckley

Ric. Parrott

Sam Lees
Gabriel Ball
Sarah Bagnall

Jno. Simpson
Ric. Cartlich
Ra. Cartlich

Hill

Geo.
Dr. Mawson
Thos.
Norbury Cartlich

Mary Dean   Wm. Burn

Thos. Lockett

Jno. Heath
Ann Cliff
Sarah Simpson
School Ho.

Tim Lockett

Paul Sheldon
P.H.

Jno. Taylor

Ric. Hume

Mrs. P.H.
Mrs. Marsh
Jno.
Drake
Thos.

Jno. Taylor
Ric. Daniel
Thos. Clews

ShoeLane
Ruffleys

Maria Lockers

S. & J. Borer
Maria
Lockers

Malk

Sam Horden

Jno. Marsh

Shord Pile

Ellen Wedgwood
Wm. Wedgwood

The Maypole

Thos.
Ditchfield

Ra. Wood
hyle

Aaron &
Little
Wedgwood

Joseph
Malkin

Thos. Fletcher

Present Ry. Sta.
entrance is 30 yds. E

castle
ewcastle

Packhorse
P.H.

Salathiel Ball

Ric. Onions

Jno. Hurd

Abner
Wedgwood

Jolly Potters
P.H.

Moses
Copeland

Ellen
Wedgwood

Moses
Marsh

Aaron
Shaw

Turks
Head
P.H.

Jane Baggaley

Thos. Procter
Timacer Daniel
Red Lion P.H.

Big Ho.

Thos. Burn

Birch Croft

Ra. Cartlich
P.H.

Wm. Allen

Jas. Plant

Smithy

Thos. Lovatt
Butcher

Blakely

Wm. Marsh

Wm. Mear
Thos. Green
Sarah Simpson
Eliz. Hall
Ric. Beech
Ric. Beech's
Smithy
Ann Bould

Jos. Hurd

Ra. Burn

John Adams
Brickhouse

Ra. Adams

Eliz. Hall

Ralph
Allen

Joseph
Marsh

Ann

Joshua
Ball

Geo. Wood
Ric. Cartright

Isa. Grundy
Cath. Wedgwood

Sam Bowers

Mary Harding

Ph. Rathbone

Martha Adams
Eliz. Ashury
Mary Brammer
Ra. Cartlich
And. Stevenson

Is. Noden

Daniel

Jonathan
Adams & Jno.
Jno.

Geo.
Dragon
Mollat

Thos.
Oldfield

Mary Gater
Jos. Marsh

Kiln Cro

Mary
Cartlich

Sam Malkin

Step. Cartlich
P.H.

rlongs

Jos. Mills

Thos.
Copeland

Bear P.H.
Jos. Adam

Thos. Needham
Sarah Stevenson

Nathan Parr
Smithy

Talbot P.H.

Jno. Daniel

Moses
Marsh

Aa. Clowes

Mansfield

Aa. Leigh

Ed.
Field

Eliz.
Barlow

Jas. Mansfield

Hy. Daniel
Thos. Simpson

Jno. Harvey

Mary Taylor

Shoulder of
Mutton P.H.

Knowle Works

Jno. Daniell
Court House P.H.

Eliz. Harvey

P.H.

Ann Ward

Jno. Ward

Ann Ward

Jno. Burn
Jos. Scarratt
Jno. Stanley
Jno. Steel

Beech's
Barn

ech's

Ed. Adams
J. & T. Taylor
Ra. Adams

Velvet Croft

Daniels Croft

Robin's Croft

Ric. Fletcher
Ric. Burn

Hole Croft

Jos. Bennet
Sam Stanley

Sam Cartlich's
Flash Works

ower Hadderidge

Upper Hadderidge

Wm. & Timothy
Lockett
Thos. Harvey

Jno. Daniel

Meadow

Aaron Cartlich

Rob!
Daniels
Holehouse Wor...

Wm. Barker

Jos. Stevens

Cross
Hill

Glebe   Lands

Thos. S...

WEDGWOOD HISTORY

*I*n the summer of 1774 fashionable ladies and gentlemen promenaded through the doors of a shop in a handsome mansion on Greek Street in London's Soho to see what would surely be the talk of tea tables and drawing rooms for the season. Here, in Josiah Wedgwood's new showrooms, was the first display of a dinner service ordered by the Empress Catherine of Russia, each piece individually and exquisitely painted, the product of three years' work. One viewer declared herself giddy at

OPPOSITE: Josiah Wedgwood was born in "The Potteries," in Staffordshire, where generations had been employed in small workshops turning out the simple tableware made from the clays and minerals found in the area. Families such as the Wedgwoods worked together, passing down the techniques and secrets of pot-making. The map depicts the densely populated area, and the distinctive cone-shaped kilns mark the potters' places.

the quantity and the quality she saw. Queen Charlotte herself would soon arrive for a viewing. Everyone noted that Mr. Wedgwood was a master.

This display represented an extraordinary journey for a man born of limited circumstances in North Staffordshire. When Josiah Wedgwood was born in 1730, ordinary people ate roughly, from a trencher and a stoneware mug, while the upper classes had their silver, gilt, and porcelain. By the time of his death English-made pottery was on tables throughout the country and abroad, products of the first major British ceramics company.

Josiah had a sense of what shoppers wanted. He helped create England's tastes, as well as forwarded the industrial revolution in England. His Enlightenment-engendered view of man's place in the world informed his work, and the company he launched and led remains, along with his notes, letters, and designs, which are drawn on by each new generation of designers and craftspeople.

A POTTER'S BEGINNINGS

Josiah Wedgwood's journey began in Burslem, a town with air smudged by the smoking kilns of small potteries producing the everyday wares for simple households. The craft and the trade arose here because the countryside yielded all that was needed—a wide variety of clays and colors, salt for glaze, coal for fires, wood for crate making. Josiah was the youngest of thirteen children born to Mary and Thomas Wedgwood; his father was a master potter who left virtually nothing when he died except a small pottery and a large family. Nine-year-old Josiah was forced to leave school and began to work for his brother Thomas at the family's Churchyard Pottery. When a smallpox epidemic swept the town, young Josiah was in bed for weeks before he recovered, scarred and limited by a painful chronic infection in his knee.

LEARNING THE TRADE

At fourteen Josiah was apprenticed to Thomas to learn "the art, mistery and occupation" of a potter. His damaged knee ensured he could no longer pump a potter's wheel, so he likely was to have learned more about the running of the company,

design, and production than was usual. The Wedgwood family had been potters for several generations, and like their competitors, borrowed, shared, or spied out the manufacturing secrets for popular new wares: salt-glazed pottery and pottery whose mineral glazes gave a marbleized effect. Improving these products became a fascination of Josiah's. Staffordshire sits on a vein of unique clays and minerals, and Josiah tried several combinations.

Thomas lacked the visionary energy of Josiah, who was alert to the changes beginning in the industry and eager to make his own contribution. The experiments were expensive, both in time and in materials, and Thomas could ill afford the research and development that interested Josiah. The brothers parted amicably, and at twenty-two Josiah began to work with other potters in Stoke-on-Trent.

In 1754 he found a partner in Thomas Whieldon, a successful potter who was equally as interested in innovation. In 1759 Josiah began to fill the first of the experiment books he kept all his life: notebooks written in a secret code to protect against prying rivals. "Everything yields to experiment," he said. He continued to experiment with glazes, trying out thousands of variations in formulas and chemical combinations.

ABOVE: "Ivy House" was Josiah Wedgwood's first factory, which he rented from his relative John Wedgwood beginning in 1769. He was said to produce salt-glazed stoneware, redware, knife handles, and lead-glazed earthenware. He had a rented wheel for turning; the two smoking chimneys show he had two ovens for his work.

THE FIRST VENTURE

In 1759 Whieldon retired and Josiah was on his own. He continued to produce objects in the rococo taste of the time: Teapots were highly decorated and brightly colored, covered in a green or mottled glaze, in fruit and vegetable shapes. Even though his work found great popularity, his goal remained to perfect the creamware that had been made in the potteries for many years. He was convinced that this material would be adaptable and salable. Finally, in 1763, he claimed credit for perfecting "a species of earthenware for the table, quite new in appearance, covered with a rich and brilliant glaze, bearing sudden alterations of heat and cold, manufactured with ease and expedition, and consequently cheap." This was elegant equipment for the home, each piece marked on the bottom with an incised "Wedgwood," at a time when potters rarely signed their work.

The business was growing; the industrial revolution was making a new stratum of wealth, a middle class of entrepreneurs and factory owners who were enamored of their new houses and popular new customs like afternoon tea. As was the usual practice in the potteries, Josiah sought a partner to complement his skills and help him grow his business. He'd met Thomas Bentley, a Liverpool merchant who was well educated and sophisticated, with a geniality and a wide-ranging mind that matched his own. When he convinced the merchant to become his partner in 1767 "and Bentley" was added to the customary "Wedgwood" stamped on the bottom of each piece.

"USEFUL AND ORNAMENTAL WARES"

Wedgwood then made two divisions for the factory's output. One division was for "Ornamental"—artistic, decorative, and high-priced—wares. These were delegated to Bentley, itemized in the agreement as being "ornamental Earthenware or Porcelain Viz Vases, Figures, Flower pots, Toylet Furniture, & such other objects as they shall from time to time agree upon." Bentley moved to London to open a shop that immediately attracted the fashionable trade.

Daily letters showed the humor, judgment, and flair for merchandising both men shared. Bentley's letters were so important to Josiah that he had them bound; the family referred to them as Josiah's bible. Topics reflected both large and small concerns: Josiah's jolly irony shows in a letter written when trade was slow: "Nobody will part with their money.—This being the case I begin my letter abusing the world & everybody in it, for a blind, sneaking, paltry, foolish world."

Fashionable ladies and gentlemen of leisure would gather at the showrooms to admire new lines and talk with the charming Mr. Bentley. Wedgwood's wares were the best—and Wedgwood charged three times the usual price. When the queen ordered a tea set painted with green flowers in 1765, she made Wedgwood & Bentley the top people's choice, too. As "Potter to the Queen," Wedgwood could add the royal coat of arms to the shop front. Josiah wrote, "The demand for this said cream colour, alias Queens Ware . . . still increases. It is really amazing how rapidly the use of it has spread almost over the whole globe."

BELOW: This receipt for an order conveys Josiah Wedgwood's growing status and appeal to the gentry. Queen Charlotte was enchanted by his creations, ordering first a tea set, then a dinner set of creamware. It became known as Queensware and has been in production for more than two centuries.

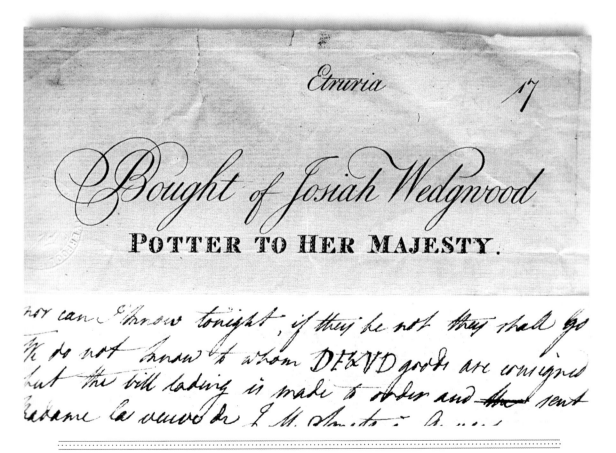

Back in Staffordshire, Josiah had taken on his first cousin Joseph as a journeyman and put him in charge of "Useful" wares, which were defined as anything for the table. There were exceptions, however; for example, very grand services like the one designed for the empress of Russia came under Bentley's supervision. Joseph's patient supervision of creamware left Josiah free for more experimenting.

THE GROWTH OF A FAMILY—AND A BUSINESS

In Josiah's time marriages were often about more than just love, so it probably wasn't surprising that he chose to wed his well-dowered distant cousin Sarah "Sally" Wedgwood in 1764. It was a perfect match; intelligent and capable, she knew the potteries well. He said that nothing left his factory unless Sally had given her opinion. "She is my chief helpmate," he wrote. As their family grew—seven babies lived—he loved to show the children chemistry experiments full of exciting bangs and smoke, and cautioned them that not to be idle was the eleventh commandment.

In 1769 the family moved to an estate he dubbed Etruria, a nod to the Etruscans; archaeological digs in Italy were revealing artifacts that sparked the fashions of Europe. The house was built in the prevailing neoclassical taste, overlooking a large new factory that was probably the finest in Europe, full of Josiah's adaptations and new technology.

A master like Joseph had both responsibility and freedom to set the rules. He disciplined workers with a posted code of conduct that barred gambling, drinking, and "obseen writing" on the walls. However, his care for workers' welfare was unique; he provided education, entertainment, and some of the earliest retirement plans. His experiments were also dedicated to removing the poisons from production, like the lead in glazes that shortened workers' lives. Josiah provided schools for their children, a library, and a "sick fund." Workers' welfare had, in fact, been a Wedgwood tradition: nine years before, John Wesley, on a tumultuous preaching tour of the potteries, had remarked, "I met a young man by the name of J. Wedgwood who planted a flower garden adjacent to his pottery. He also has his men wash their hands and faces and change their clothes after working in the clay. He is small and lame but his soul is close to God."

THE POWER OF INVENTION

"I have many ideas & visions crowd in upon me, not only quicker than I can execute them, but faster than I can find time to lay them to rest a while in my Common Place Book," Josiah wrote. The new house had a hidden workroom, safe from prying eyes and imitators who put out reasonable copies.

His first search was for "black basalt," a version of black stoneware. It allowed the firm to offer wares from medallions to vases in the neoclassical tradition and prompted large orders by 1769.

It took more than ten thousand trial pieces to perfect jasper—Wedgwood called it a "whimsical" substance—with success not totally achieved until 1777. A white stoneware fired at a slightly higher than normal temperature, it could be glazed or tinted in tones like blue and green. The crisp modeling and dramatic contrast of white figures on a colored background delighted the eye. With a few gaps, jasper has stayed in production for more than two centuries.

Now the refined designs of the classical potters could be reproduced in a manner to please the new collectors. There were many forms, often in shapes the Etruscans never knew—bulb pots, for instance, or teapots. Josiah's pottery innovations were perfectly timed for the newest fashion that affected everything from door knobs to ladies' dresses: the taste for the neoclassical, which was known as the "true" or "correct" style. The excavations at Herculaneum and Pompeii in the mid-eighteenth century had brought the interest to a peak. Neoclassical interiors and possessions lent polish, sophistication, and historical references to their owners.

In 1763 Josiah had created something new to English pottery—the ornamental

Admission to see Mr Wedgwood's Copy of
THE PORTLAND VASE

Greek Street, Soho, between 12 o'Clock and 5

ABOVE: The public's excitement was overwhelming when Josiah Wedgwood announced his reproduction of The Portland Vase—a blue glass ancient Roman vase, cameo-cut, once owned by the Duke of Portland, and made in the Augustan era. Wedgwood translated the beauty of the glass into his own deep blue jasper with classical figures in white applied to the service. Extraordinary craftsmanship and a high price meant only a few were produced, with the first perfect examples appearing in 1789.

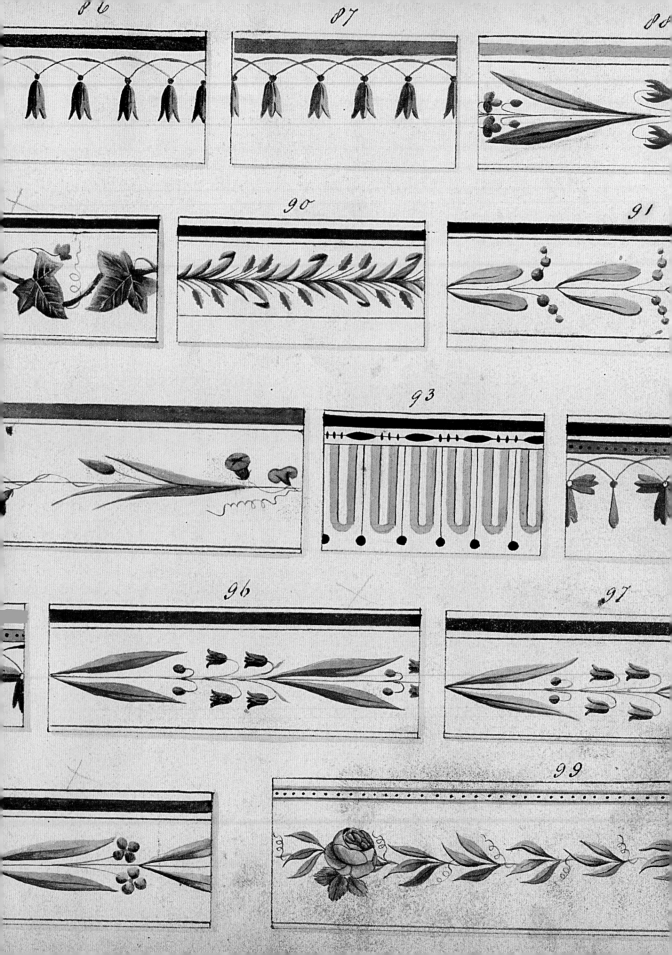

vase, sparking what became known as "vase-mania." Inspired by the ancient Greek and Roman vases that were used to hold oil or water, Wedgwood vases were strictly for viewing, the crowning touch to a shelf or a mantelpiece. By 1777 he had more than a hundred different shapes available. Sally wrote: "My good man is on the ramble continually and I am almost affraid he wil [*sic*] layout the price of his estate in Vases." He titled himself "Vase maker general to the universe," and after a visit to the London showrooms his sister reported that there was "no Getting to the door for coaches nor into the rooms for ladies & gentn & vases . . . vases was all the cry."

WEDGWOOD AND THE WORLD

Wedgwood and Bentley's first catalog appeared in 1773 with long lists of plaques, candlesticks, and vases picturing every god and goddess from mythology—and the worthies of Josiah's own era—that could be purchased. Did a customer want an image of Apollo or Isaac Newton? Both were available. Independent artists were commissioned to produce exactly what Josiah wanted, like the romantic designs full of frisking putti drawn by society belles such as Lady Diana Beauclerk and Lady Elizabeth Templetown; he had his own specially trained painters and molders, too.

Wedgwood wasn't sold exclusively to the British even in Josiah's time; many of his wares were earmarked for shipment abroad. Creamware and the neoclassical designs found an immediate audience. The aristocracy of the New World drew their culture directly from England, and travel back and forth was encouraged. Meal patterns and tea traditions were similar, and education was classically based. Many of the values of the blooming democracy were drawn from ancient Greece and its philosophers, so choosing a neoclassical piece had political overtones. (Though a Philadelphian was predictably cautious, saying of her new jasper tea set with its frolicking nymphs, "We thought the little creatures should have been cloathed," lest a guest's "delicacy" be harmed.)

THE LATER YEARS

By now, Josiah himself had accrued the hallmarks of a gentleman. The 1780 family portrait by George Stubbs shows the children dressed in silks and fine linen, while Sally, in a hat overflowing with feathers, takes her ease at her husband's side. As Josiah aged, he took more time at home with his children, reading with them at breakfast, talking to Sally, and working in his experiment room.

He remained energetic and curious. He was now a peer, and a friend, of other gentlemen marked by energy and inquiry, joining with Joseph Priestley, Erasmus Darwin, James Watt, and others in Birmingham's Lunar Society, named for the nights they chose to dine, when the full moon lit the way home. They discussed the affairs of the day and the scientific conundrums each was pondering—Priestley's chemistry or Watt's steam experiments—and corresponded with others of their ilk in France and America. Josiah, whose religious background was Unitarian, with its emphasis on inquiry and social responsibility, believed strongly in the rights of man, supporting both the American and the French revolutions, however badly the situation affected his trade. In one downturn, he wrote to Bentley that he was "feeling just now very chagrinish at being stopped in my career, and not permitted to proceed in the invention of new pots and pipkins for my own amusement first, and afterwards for the emolument and entertainment of all the world." Josiah was a prime mover in modernization, especially when it helped his endeavors, and he offered

BELOW: The exquisite care taken by Josiah Wedgwood in his experiments meant thousands of trials were made for each new development. These jasper color swatches show the different effects of adjusting temperature, position, and time in the oven. Wedgwood's blues were especially sought after. Jasper is considered the potter's greatest triumph and was immediately popular.

robust support for the new Trent and Mersey Canal; completed in 1777, it helped businesses ship their goods with less damage. Having been careful to buy land next to the proposed route, he positioned his factory there.

CHANGING TIMES

Josiah Wedgwood died in 1795 and left his family an enormous legacy—property, money, reputation, and a thriving business. Seeing a natural heir in his son Josiah II, he had fostered the young man's interest in the company. Josiah II did not see himself as a potter in the Staffordshire smoke; like many sons of famous fathers, he needed to find his own place. He had established himself as a country squire in Surrey. Upright and starchy, he lacked his father's easy charm. But the factory could not continue without a strong visionary at its head, and as business faltered, he stepped up to the leadership role in 1805. He perfected a Wedgwood bone china in 1812 and did his best to improve the legacy of design that was the company's heritage. When Josiah II retired in 1845, his son Josiah III came into the company. As the nineteenth century progressed, more young men of the family joined the firm.

The next boom arrived when the Victorians found Wedgwood to be a good source of pretty things for the parlor as well as the huge tableware sets their dining style required. Majolica was a great success in the last half of the nineteenth century. The pieces were painted in gleaming deep hues, with figures taken from mythology, botany, and zoology—here a lobster, there a lily—or all three. "Art pottery" was developed in response to the new arts and crafts and aesthetic movements, with their emphasis on handcraft and natural and historical themes. Painted porcelain was considered a branch of fine art and was collected by connoisseurs; artists such as the illustrator and author Walter Crane, a leading figure of the arts and crafts movement and friend of William Morris, worked for the company. The production line reflected each passing art movement: sinuously painted pieces during the art nouveau period, Japanese motifs when Asia was in vogue, and mob-capped moppets when Kate Greenaway was popular.

Tableware poured from the factory to meet the demand of the Victorians, who set their tables for many courses, with dishes shaped to just one use, whether for celery or cream soup. The engine of income that was the British Empire meant more and more households could afford the Wedgwood productions. The cult of the home emphasized that a proper life required a vast flotilla of accessories, from sets of china for the washstand to decorative busts for the library. Exports to Europe and beyond also stretched the impact of Wedgwood wares, which became necessities on tea tables in Australia and the Canadian west.

By the turn of the century, hard times had begun again. Taste is cyclical, responsive to changing conditions, and the public was now surfeited with lavish decoration, while wars and worry around the globe affected exports. In 1904 Wedgwood hired John Goodwin to be director of design. He went back to the roots of Wedgwood design and revived eighteenth-century shapes and creamware. The clean design was refreshing to shoppers after half a century of pieces that emphasized lavish decoration, and was perhaps a comfort to populations uncertain about the future and longing for what seemed a noble and stable past.

The thirties depression taxed the company, with exports severely affected by the global setbacks. Design, however, hit one of its high notes; for the first time, the company hired an art director: the visionary Victor Skellern, who would develop the look of Wedgwood for more than thirty years. "There is no such thing as traditional or contemporary design," he explained. "These are merely convenient labels. Design is either good or bad: if good, it lasts; if bad, it doesn't."

Modernism was on the march, and Wedgwood found some of the best practitioners to turn their hands to designs for new forms and decoration. The first Josiah himself might have liked the clean line and harmony of form produced by designers like Keith Murray. A New Zealander trained as an architect, he designed simple tablewares and vases that were unadorned except by flawless new glazes and perhaps some machine turning. In the pacesetting Royal Academy exhibition of 1935, Wedgwood's wares were the most represented, and Murray's designs were acclaimed. Many were produced well into the Fifties, and are collectors' gold today.

Pieces by watercolorist Eric Ravilious seem to summon up the long summer days in the years before World War II, with their idyllic visions of country and city, done in his distinctive style, sharp and unsentimental, derived from his skills as an engraver. He then became a war artist and was, poignantly, lost on a mission. His pieces, too, appeal today, for their halcyon mood and amusing themes of joyous days.

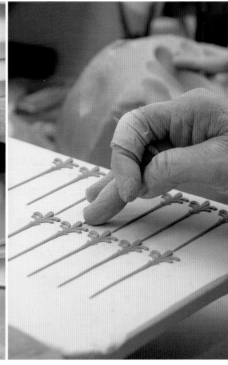

CONTEMPORARY WEDGWOOD

Design at Wedgwood remains especially important today because a love of good design is global. Wedgwood's independent designers have often made a splash in another field like interior decorating or fashion, and the alliance with Wedgwood allows them to bring new ideas to the company; Vera Wang and Jasper Conran are two examples.

Wedgwood has faced challenges throughout the centuries. Josiah and his followers appreciated the effects of changing tastes, wars and shortages, and new ways of living. The company, now a presence in most of the countries around the world, still innovates to suit its clientele: In Japan, where gift giving is so important in business and personal lives, the prestige lines of decorative accessories like clocks, vases, and ceremonial urns are in demand. In Italy and Holland, Edme, which is celebrating its hundredth year in production, is still the most popular pattern. Soup tureens sell in Europe, while tea sets are popular

ABOVE LEFT: Wedgwood riches are kept in vaults with the molds, and some shapes have developed over the course of two centuries and have never been out of production, their unending appeal defining a classic.

ABOVE CENTER: Impeccable craftsmanship, like these teapot lids waiting for the kiln, for example, are what make Wedgwood pieces timeless.

ABOVE RIGHT: With ease that comes from experience, a woman tamps clay into a shallow mold of fleur de lys, which will be affixed to a jasper urn. They have been made in the same way for two hundred years. In the Potteries, one senses tradition and the pride it engenders, in the skills that are so similar to those Josiah Wedgwood himself knew.

again all over the world. The American market's strength is in the traditional bridal registry.

Contemporary habits—the decline of the sit-down dinner, hurried lives, less space reserved for storage, even cleanup with a dishwasher and cooking in a microwave—have also affected what's needed for the table. Wedgwood has responded to today's needs with their adaptable designs for comtemporary living.

WEDGWOOD DESIGNERS PAST AND PRESENT

JASPER CONRAN

GEORGE DAVES

ERIC RAVILIOUS

LADY TEMPLETOWN

SUSIE COOPER

VERA WANG

EMILE LESSORE

Getting the message to shoppers was Josiah Wedgwood's forte; his ability to sense change and to keep a step ahead of fashion was unmatched. The company still has that challenge in mind. Lord Wedgwood, who travels widely to meet Wedgwood enthusiasts, says he sees a new interest and the importance of a nicely set table, candlelight, and a conversation. "Don't save the best for another day," he'll say to them, appreciating that the art of the table, and time together, is the real gift that's timeless.

JOHN FLAXMAN

JOSIAH WEDGWOOD

MARTHA STEWART

MARTIN HUNT   DAVID QUEENSBURY

BARBARA BARRY

KEITH MURRAY

BEATRIX POTTER

INSPIRED BY THE PAST

SOME OF US COME TO LOVE WEDGWOOD THROUGH INHERITANCE OR MEMORY—
THOUGHTS OF A SUNDAY LUNCH, OR A TEAPOT FROM A GRANDMOTHER. SOME SIMPLY
APPRECIATE WEDGWOOD'S BEAUTY AND HISTORY. FOR COLLECTORS PROFILED IN THIS
BOOK, WEDGWOOD IS AN EXPRESSION OF THEIR PERSONAL STYLE AND LOVE FOR SETTING
A FINE TABLE. SOME LOVE THE BEST EIGHTEENTH-CENTURY PIECES, OTHERS MIX VINTAGE
AND MODERN, AND SOME USE CONTEMPORARY WARES. WHAT THEY ALL HAVE IN
COMMON, OF COURSE, IS A LOVE OF WEDGWOOD.

CAROLYNE ROEHM
A MOVEABLE FEAST

Carolyne Roehm is one of the bright lights in the big city, glittering at formal evenings and benefits, a favorite friend of a whole constellation of New Yorkers and beyond. At ease anywhere—she recently returned from sailing around Cape Horn—it's at Weatherstone, her fifty-nine-acre Connecticut estate where, she says, "I just come in the gate and I feel at peace, at home." She keeps her horses here, and gardens stretch in all directions, with flowers to be brought into the house for Carolyne to create one of the abundant arrangements that she made the subject of the first of her six books about living with style. An art major in college, then a fashion designer, she has both a fine eye and deep expertise.

OPPOSITE: The opulence of the understated is expressed in the painted plates, which are pleasing to both a modern and a Georgian eye. Josiah Wedgwood established a training school for his young painters so that they could learn to fulfill his exacting requirements. Customers could individualize their orders by choosing their own colors and patterns.

RIGHT AND BELOW RIGHT: Fine eighteenth-century creamware has hand-painted blue designs. A tureen has a finial, or "knop," in a flower-bud shape; Wedgwood made a wide variety of finial shapes according to period: acorns, a Sibyl, a flower blossom. A sugar caster partners the plates; spring bulbs bloom in little barklike vases by Ted Muehling. Blue and white Murano glasses complete the table.

OPPOSITE: In what was once a formal dining room, Carolyne has dressed the table for spring, using her favorite color scheme of blue and white—the subject of her latest book, *A Passion for Blue and White*.

Weatherstone has known heartbreak: Almost ten years ago, the house, built in 1765, caught fire and the roof collapsed, finishing off a world-class collection of art and antiques. "But my china and my cooking pots were saved and I was so grateful," says Carolyne. She moved into the carriage house and thought carefully about what she loved and what she needed. Two years later, she'd re-created the house, preserving its heritage but opening up the spaces into a lofty, airy place where the sun pours in. "It was time for a design that drew more from the pale furniture and sensibility of northern countries like Scandinavia, not brown English furniture and acres of chintz," she explained. She introduced a mix that matches—French and Swedish and German antiques, as well as English pieces—and mirrors everywhere bounce the light and sparkle. The atmosphere is calm, spacious, pared down; the luxury lavished by soft upholstery, books to read, and

OPPOSITE: In autumn, country comforts demand a seat by the fire after a walk in the fiery-leafed woods. A William IV round table is set for a few good friends with eighteenth-century plates; in the center are flowers in a period tureen painted with oak leaves and acorns, which symbolize strength and fortitude.

views from the windows that sweep across the Connecticut countryside.

Carolyne takes advantage of every nook of the house when entertaining. "I'd had a huge formal dining room, but, though I enjoyed being able to serve a large group for a dinner, it was just a passageway most of the time." Now dining is a movable feast—she'll pull a table close to a fireplace (there are eleven in the house to choose from), bring in chairs and her monogrammed linens, and inspect the range of cupboards that hold china of every mood and description to see what works for the occasion. "Living in every part of your house resembles the way it was done in the eighteenth century. Rooms served many purposes, as use demanded," she says.

"I am to china what Imelda Marcos was to shoes," she adds with a laugh. "I find it difficult not to fall in love when I see something wonderful, and to bring it home. I can barely pass the windows of Bardith in Manhattan without stopping. I see things I can't resist. They sell the best and have perfect examples of fine Wedgwood. And I use everything I own."

Carolyne found the shell-edged blue and white Wedgwood china twenty years ago and has been adding to it whenever she finds a piece. There are fine plates and tureens that can stand on their own as centerpieces, as well as other serving dishes. "They are so sculptural; they make wonderful decoration," she explains. A connoisseur of these eighteenth-century wares, she prizes their workmanship and the feel of each object in her hand. "And I've always been drawn to blue and white combinations," she adds. "Every culture has had its blue and white decor, from the early Chinese porcelain to Dutch and English delft and Persian and other Islamic art." She sets the table by interweaving all these threads of history and taste for a one-of-a-kind tabletop that tells its own story.

SENSE

AND

SENSIBILITY:

A NOVEL.

IN THREE VOLUMES.

BY A LADY.

VOL. I.

London:

PRINTED FOR THE AUTHOR,

THE GREYFRIAR

SUIVANT SAINT PIERRE

JANE AUSTEN
SENSE AND SENSIBILITY

One day in 1811 a bonneted woman joined the throng of shoppers at the Wedgwood showroom in London, hoping to add some pieces to her family's collection. Her mother had requested replacement pieces for their china with its pattern of leaves. Later, at home in Hampshire, Jane Austen unpacked the new china and deemed it a good match, though with her usual humor she suggested, "I think they might have allowed us rather larger leaves, especially in such a Year of fine foliage as this."

The little family—Jane; her sister, Cassandra; and their widowed mother—had moved into a cottage in the small village of Chawton in 1809.

OPPOSITE, ABOVE LEFT AND BELOW RIGHT: On display at Chawton Cottage are pieces from the grand china service Edward Austen Knight ordered in 1813. It was suitable for his life in the landed gentry, where elaborate dinners, served in late afternoon, were part of the rituals of the wealthy, followed by tea and dances, with family and neighbors of sufficient social standing.

OPPOSITE, BELOW LEFT: Jane accompanied Edward to the Wedgwood showroom in London to place the china order. The crest depicted a Greyfriar monk like the one seen today on the local pub sign across the road.

The Austens were to live there quietly, a model of Regency gentility, with rounds of visiting, letter writing, sewing, and chores to fill their days. And then there was Jane, sitting in the parlor and writing her stories in her neat hand. Here, from this secluded village, she sent her novels out into the world.

The substantial cottage belonged to her brother Edward. He had been adopted by Thomas and Catherine Knight, childless and wealthy cousins who were charmed by him; he inherited their estates, including Chawton Great House. He ensured his mother's and sisters' peaceful existence by moving them into the cottage. The three Austen women lived in reduced circumstances; a widow and two unmarried daughters had very little to subsist on but their pride and the customs they had formed in brighter days. A Wedgwood breakfast set was her mother's joy, and Jane, whose job it was to prepare tea each morning, would have used the pot for the first of the day's cups, then probably washed it carefully by hand herself, though they had a servant.

Though she did not like the smoky city and its rush, she did enjoy it when wealthy Henry sent her off in his carriage to do the errands for Cassandra and her mother—shopping for a bonnet, a ribbon, a length of fabric, or their tea.

Edward invited her to come along when he and his daughter Fanny chose the new Wedgwood dinner service for his house. After the visit to Wedgwood's shop, where Edward placed his order, Jane described it in a letter to the family at home: "the pattern is a small Lozenge in purple, between Lines of narrow Gold;—& it is to have the Crest."

And so the Knight order appears in the Wedgwood records, with a list that includes, among the 167 pieces, "Etruscan soup tureens" and six dozen table plates, pickle saucers and a fish drainer, "root dishes" in the "French" style, and a gravy dish. Visit the Austen house in Chawton to see a few pieces from the set, still the picture of elegant refinement.

THOMAS O'BRIEN
VINTAGE MODERN

One early-summer afternoon, Thomas O'Brien, out of town on business, called some of his good friends. "My garden's at its best. You've got to see it. Take some wine and go watch the sunset!" he said from a faraway hotel room. And so they did, watching the gilded Long Island light on the nodding early roses, sharing the largesse of his perfect house filled with all the things he loves. Thomas's home is on a part of Long Island that draws those who want a quieter refuge than the oh-so-hot Hamptons. It's a small seaside town with romantic appeal—lanes wind to the ocean, shadowed by tall old trees; turreted Victorian houses stand next to those from the seventeenth century; and sailboats bob in the bay.

OPPOSITE: When Wedgwood produced these Adam plates in 1879, they recaptured the taste for a neoclassical detail of swags and cameos but treated them completely differently. The stemware is from the American Heisey factory, with dimpled Russell Wright green tumblers.

ABOVE: O'Brien designed this long table just for informal meals. He sweeps his books to one end, then sets the table with easy elegance, making an everyday meal special—and giving himself another chance to use what he loves. Formal plays against casual with the Adam plate juxtaposed with vintage Gorham cutlery. The early-nineteenth-century Wedgwood creamware bowl in the background holds old linen napkins; Thomas says this is the piece he uses the most, loving its quiet elegance and adaptability.

RIGHT: With more pieces in his collections than surfaces to display them, Thomas makes a still life on the mantelpiece of an assortment of objects, then switches them as he pleases. His collections, he says, are both a passion and an obsession—there is no "enough." Arrangements like this let him enjoy everything. Organization comes from a rhythm of form and color. "It all has to do with the geometry of a piece," he says. A green glass vase connects to a green shagreen cup and saucer and the verdigris of the bronze fawn. The Wedgwood basalt jug here is an old form reminiscent of the same neoclassical taste as the antique bust and the dulled-silver candlestick; its bowl resembles an ancient goblet. The black and white scientific study of sea life provides a graphic background.

Here, in this quiet village, Thomas, a top designer with a thriving practice and a pacesetting shop, bought an 1833 schoolhouse and transformed it into a comfortable home, where he weekends away from his New York apartment. The old school afforded him the light-filled sweeping spaces he loves, which, painted in whites and pale tints of color, are backdrops for his real trove—the multitude of objects he has accumulated over the years, including a serious collection of vintage and eighteenth-century Wedgwood.

It would be easy to say Thomas is a collector. And he is, but to a degree most can't match. Typically, his eye leads and his heart follows. Some things are valuable, others not so. One is rarely enough. Multiples, please, and often the serendipity of flea markets and yard sales cast up more of what he covets, in a way he dubs spooky. He is unstoppable—he stores objects he doesn't have room to display and has just bought the house next door as an annex.

Luckily, his sense of proportion and of discipline lend structure to his rooms and guide his decorating. It can take a moment to understand why his many possessions live so harmoniously and don't just seem like a tidal wave of beautiful objects that swirl around the space. Instead, a visitor immediately recognizes the beauty of the room, then begins to identify individual objects that have interesting shapes or history, then spots the way each is enhanced by the next object. Sometimes it's color, sometimes it's the silhouette ("which is so important"), sometimes it's an allusion to his past or to a lost era. And an assortment of furniture in tones of cream, gray, and deep woods also serves as a reticent frame. Thomas's own tendencies toward order are also helpful—he knows where everything is and cannot bear disorganization.

"I like to call the way I decorate 'vintage modern,'" he says,

and his atelier in Manhattan, Aero, has been a leader in the fashionable appetite for mixing the past and the present, to create a whole new style. When he sets a table, there is no matching all-of-a-piece effect. His use of Wedgwood illustrates this clearly; the company has constantly referenced its elegant past as it enters a new era, and pieces of Wedgwood from diverse eras give him many reference points.

In this informal lunch, served at a long table in his open living room, Thomas chose plates in Adam, a pattern developed in 1850 that nodded to the neoclassical motifs that were Josiah Wedgwood's stock in trade but with considerably more decoration. The muted colors of the plate relate to the table's glassware, which was made a hundred years later: Russell Wright's quiet green tumblers from the 1950s. The Wedgwood creamware dish in faux basket weave from c. 1810 sustains the simple elegance. Tactile details also unite the table—soft damask napkins, heavy vintage cutlery, some black basalt with its distinctive surface, a favorite stone sculpture of a seal.

"I feel it's all quite modern, really, the restraint, the lack of extraneous decoration—it's so crisp," he says. Thomas's love of china is unending: "I had one plate of Pagoda that I just loved." But with just one, he used it as a starting point for setting the table with a motley of pretty but single examples of plates. Then he happened upon a whole set of Pagoda—and snapped it up.

"It's part of the journey of collecting," he says.

He likes the resonance of the past that comes with vintage things, whether it's the aura that stems from his own memory or the tale that is half told by a newly bought object. "Who loved this? Who lost it? Where has it been? I am

TOP AND OPPOSITE: A weekend breakfast for houseguests is an occasion to pull out the Wedgwood set of Summer Sky china. Its unadorned forms were made in post-war England, when the nation was just emerging from restrictions. The blue reflects the optimism of the period.

ABOVE: Even when Thomas is not entertaining, his pieces stand ready, like the Wedgwood mugs. They are by Keith Murray, a much-collected 1930s designer whose inspired interpretation of modernist themes has made them timeless. Thomas uses even precious objects for daily pleasure. "What's most important to me are the stories, the places these objects had in past lives," he says.

RIGHT: Keith Murray is one of Thomas's favorite Wedgwood designers. Even though these 1930s bowls are valuable, Thomas uses them every day. "Nothing is too precious to use," he believes.

OPPOSITE: The necklaces in jasper are related to the time when eighteenth-century ladies and gentlemen used Wedgwood's jasper medallions to decorate their dresses and hairstyles. These came from one of Thomas's strolls through an online auction searching for new things.

CENTER: Thomas has also been lucky in antiques shops. Piles of Wedgwood plates in Pagoda were a find from a local shop.

always so curious about an object's past life before it came to me." Even when there's no way to know, the object is invested with that past. He'll label a piece "interesting" or "intriguing" rather than valuable or pretty. "I like to learn about the history of things," he explains, "like the Wedgwood creamware, or Eric Ravilious, the thirties painter who created so many charming pieces for them." Sometimes, though, the history is personal. His arrangements can almost seem like a little playlet. Look at the collection of objects on his chest of drawers: a very precious Wedgwood engine-turned bowl from iconic 1930s designer Keith Murray, a vivid turquoise Roycroft vase, an early-twentieth-century portrait of a sad-eyed child, a vintage wristwatch. The creamy color is a link, with the jolt of blue, so it isn't boring. And what of the child's eyes, so haunting, with one of Thomas's handkerchiefs on a stand before it? A collector who

relied on guidebooks and prices at auction would never inject an emotive context to these things, as Thomas has done.

Each of his arrangements has its internal rhyme scheme, and is limitlessly—or almost—expandable. "I like the oddest things, I know," he admits. "I am always looking, shopping, finding—with the Internet I can in the middle of the night—and everything I bring home does flow together and find its home in a group of objects."

And so he'll set the table with an assortment of things that speak to one another, though their origins may span centuries: A Victorian Wedgwood dinner plate and the fifties glass might seem distant, but each complements the other, the simple, sober shape of the glass toning down the swags and medallions of the plate, the plate tempering the gravity of the glass.

CHARLOTTE MOSS
MIDNIGHT SUPPER

*I*t's late evening and, back from the ballet, Manhattan designer Charlotte Moss pours the wine for a midnight supper with her husband. She's using her collection of antique and modern Wedgwood pieces to set the table in a black and white color scheme as classic as a dinner jacket, turning a simple supper into a feast for the senses. "I love the clarity of old Wedgwood designs," she says of this table that mixes black basalt with creamware, the black of the basalt glowing against the delicate color of the plates on the soft pink tablecloth.

Though Charlotte Moss knows how to invest an everyday moment with seemingly effortless glamour, she is not the woman of leisure that skill might imply.

OPPOSITE: A table placed before the fire is draped with shell-pink linens. White and pale pink anenomes fill a pastille burner from Wedgwood's Prestige collection. A charger and smaller plates in Wedgwood White and snowy linens with Charlotte's monogram bring light to the table, along with the glimmer of glassware and silver in the firelight.

ABOVE LEFT: A place setting rests on the chair as Charlotte sets the table.

ABOVE RIGHT: Bouquets of anenomes fill black basalt jugs and vases to create the table's focal point.

RIGHT: This black basalt bowl is decorated with a frieze of nymphs in the neoclassical taste.

She works hard, as she has all her life. Once she worked on Wall Street; then she married an investment banker and turned her hand to decorating her houses in a style that combined luxury, historicity, and wit. It wasn't long before the compliments turned into requests from others to design their own houses—or to design sheets, or fabrics, or tea sets—all marked with the innate style that's informed by her knowledge and experience. Twice, in some of the toniest parts of New York, she has even opened walk-in-and-marvel stores showcasing goods that illustrate her sense of home. Managing to combine the cozy and the grand, the shops were the perfect place to find a small present, like something as simple as a dozen bamboo plates for a picnic or as elaborate as a bed and all the lavish linens to outfit it. The shops were perfect renderings of Charlotte's wide-ranging interests and constant curiosity.

ABOVE: A linen napkin with Charlotte's monogram complements her basalt and creamware plates. She loves the versatility of these dishes because "you can mix and match and add over the years, layer and adapt."

Born in Richmond, Charlotte remains the quick-witted and warm blonde whose ready curiosity led her to New York and her careers. One of five children in a close family, she had a grandmother in the neighborhood who passed on the importance of living well and taught her the fine points along the way. Her knowledge of china came from this grandmother: "It was a special day when my mother would take me to see my grandmother, who managed the china department at Miller and Rhoads," she recalls. "It was the downtown department store with the kind of tearoom where lucky little girls in nice dresses were taken to lunch in an atmosphere of ladylike joys. "We'd order chicken salad in a pineapple—you know, typical South—and watch a fashion show. At home, she'd always have me help set the table, so I learned from an early age.

"Of course, I feel like I've known about Wedgwood my whole life. And then, I collect, and always have. We were a family that liked to entertain, and I still love it, and the china that goes with it. And I knew that our dinners 'round the table were precious—I was raised knowing that mealtime was important, and that all five of us were expected to be at the table every night."

Those family dinners did leave her with a hunger for wonderful china and a determination to perpetuate those moments around the table, with all their humor and warmth. "Fixing up the table is one of those examples of everyday decorating when you can have so much fun! I've got lots to choose from. I am always on the lookout for great china. I bought some of Wedgwood's bright green leaf plates long ago and added and added. But I don't need a complete set of anything—if I've only got six of something, that's what I'll use.

"When I see something that appeals to me, I ask myself, 'Do I need it?' Uh, no. So then I ask myself, 'How much do I love it, and what can go with it?' That's the answer I listen to." She is always prepared to invite someone for dinner, lunch, or tea, with closets full of napkins ironed and waiting, glassware polished, and then she lets her imagination roam as she sets the table.

"I like flexibility in people—and in china," she says. "I love creamware because it's so adaptable. It can be the star of a

table, or a contrast to another piece. I love basalt, the texture, the color, the history," she says. This black/white/pink scheme was inspired "by Madeleine Castaing's bathroom," she says, citing the innovative and elegant Parisian decorator whose own style was a mix of the neoclassical and the eccentric. "I like to use contemporary china for every day, like Wedgwood's cream-ware, which is so easily adaptable," Charlotte says. "And then I have a collection of some real treasures, eighteenth-century pieces, that I use as accents. Two enormous eighteenth-century tureens. Two little footed jardinieres. I like all the specialty pieces Wedgwood designed."

She never runs out of ideas—or energy. But setting an inviting table is not a chore; it's a pleasure. "Set a table with flair, and you honor yourself, and you honor your guest."

CHRISTINE MALY
AN EDITED SELECTION

Old wood, antique china, a harmony of tone and shape—when Christine Maly sets her table, she lets the pieces she loves speak for themselves, whether a Chippendale chair or a Wedgwood plate; this isn't about matching but about harmony. "It does take an eye," she admits. "But I can't rest until everything is arranged so it looks good, even if I'm eating alone. I go by the old saying 'Good taste can be taught, but beauty is felt.'" And the feeling Christine produces with every new setting is peace and a tranquil beauty.

As Bloomingdale's Fashion Director for Tabletop, Christine first fell in love with Wedgwood creamware on her business trips to London.

OPPOSITE: The formula for caneware, a bisque made from colored marl (clay), was one of the most difficult to create. Josiah and his son Josiah II experimented for twenty years to perfect it at the end of the eighteenth century. These plates, embossed with leaves in the characteristic straw color, are late Victorian. Many drabware motifs, like bamboo or woven reeds, are derived from nature. Christine likes to add pieces such as this, still in natural colors but with pattern, to mix with the plain creamware.

"I can't stop looking, even when I think my shelves are full. I'll stop the car for garage sales, as well as London antiques stores. I've been on rain-soaked fields in the north of England, and at Bermondsey Market in London when even the birds aren't up." She loves the hunt, not only for treasures but for all she learns along the way. "I'll go looking for creamware, then find these very interesting plates with the leaves on them in a curious sort of tan. Marked Wedgwood, so I knew they were good.

"Today we don't have just one correct way to set a table. You can mix patterns, eras, and colors, and some of the newer designers, like Barbara Barry and Jasper Conran, make sets that lend themselves to this free-form way of putting together a place setting. Just make it all flow together by using a narrow range of colors, or pick a theme—I like things with designs drawn from nature. Composition is all about shapes, form, the relationships among things, and experimenting to find that what's most important is what's pleasing to you."

ABOVE LEFT: A grand cupboard, a fine Chippendale armchair, and a large eighteenth-century Wedgwood creamware platter demonstrate the period's attention to design: simple, balanced, and ageless.

ABOVE RIGHT: The sunflower embossed on the drabware plate is a design much favored by the aesthetic movement at the end of the nineteenth century, which was heavily influenced by Japanese art. The fashionable set flocked to buy such dessert plates in 1880.

OPPOSITE: The new silver-plate teakettle (inspired by Edwardian spirit kettles) is from the Barbara Barry collection at Wedgwood. The 1920s cream teacups are embossed with ivy and vines; botanical motifs have never faded in Britain.

STEPHEN DRUCKER
LITERARY FIGURES

When Stephen Drucker, the editor in chief of *House Beautiful*, began to plan his new apartment, he knew the focal point would be his prized collection of Wedgwood black basalt portrait busts—also known as The Boys. The Boys have been with him since a mind-altering moment in New York's Doyle auction galleries. "I had been living in an apartment that was all English-eccentric. I wanted to redo it, but I had no vision for it." When he entered the gallery's sale room and saw the lot of four busts of famous authors in black basalt, however, he was impressed. Milton, Byron, Burns, Shakespeare—he recognized both the models and the method; Josiah Wedgwood had used his new black basalt ware in the

OPPOSITE: A basalt wine ewer is an exquisite and precious example of Wedgwood craftsmanship and style. It illustrates the neoclassical ideal of refined ornament. On Stephen's wall is a collection of five hundred reproduction plaster casts that he amassed online; perfect framing makes them come alive, as does the careful display.

eighteenth century to portray the heroes of the day. I was completely won over. A day later, they were mine." Part of the appeal was pure aesthetics and history: "The drama of their black basalt and fine carving, and the masculinity, and the reminder of the Grand Tour, when these were the sorts of souvenirs people looked for in Italy." And part was intellectual: "I admire the age of the Enlightenment, when being educated was something to be aspired to, with busts like these in a gentleman's library."

Adopting The Boys gave Stephen a plan for his new apartment, a way of organizing everything from color to furniture, when less was definitely more appealing. He cites the old decorating rule that every room needs a touch of black. "Strength and structure set the pace of any room," he avows. "But I don't think you need much else with the busts on display on their Colefax and Fowler brackets. The busts are very adaptable and can live anywhere, whether they're put on a good Gillows

ABOVE: With the beautifully modeled bust of the eighteenth-century actor-playwright David Garrick at the left, The Boys are good examples of Wedgwood's portrait busts in black basalt. The "library busts" were an eighteenth-century enthusiasm revived in the late nineteenth century.

OPPOSITE, ABOVE: A gray cashmere throw complements an assortment of small busts, a silhouette, and an Hermès quizzing glass.

OPPOSITE, BELOW: Some of Stephen's most precious objects are displayed on a green tole bookcase. The bowl with the festoons and engine-turned lines is a classic example of Wedgwood's rich but reticent design. The boat-shaped oil lamp was Stephen's first purchase of basalt.

OPPOSITE, ABOVE LEFT: The viola de gamba vase is rare, dating to the early nineteenth century.

OPPOSITE, ABOVE RIGHT: While imitations of Roman originals were made, much more popular were the portrayals of respected authors like Dante.

OPPOSITE, BELOW LEFT: The fine execution of the Garrick bust dates it to the earliest period of Wedgwood production—around 1775. Molded, not carved, the bust's flawless detail shows the skill of the craftspeople. Byron exemplifies the era's ideal romantic hero.

OPPOSITE, BELOW RIGHT: In the lines at its base the bowl demonstrates the engine turning invented by Josiah Wedgwood in 1763. The ability to do such fine work was enhanced by his invention of a machine that held the cutting tool straight while the piece revolved around it. A descendant of that machine is still in use at Wedgwood.

Regency bookcase or something from Crate and Barrel."

Black basalt busts like these were among Josiah Wedgwood's major successes. They met the rising fancy for such emblematic objects that came with the enthusiasm for classical sculpture—the Romans had been the first to make portrait busts. Their popularity also stemmed from the Enlightenment-bred sense of the importance of the individual. Though Josiah produced some images that had obvious Roman links, such as a fine image of Mercury, he was as likely to offer the worthies of the day done in Roman style. His 1787 catalog lists ninety busts of subjects ranging from scientists to politicians.

Known as "library busts," they were made to be placed on a shelf or on the pediment of a desk or on a table, lending a bit of gravitas by establishing the owner as a man with heroes who made their reputations elsewhere than the battlefield. The busts were still produced into the twentieth century, when Winston Churchill and the queen were immortalized this way.

"I'd always liked basalt," Stephen says. "It's mysterious in a way; the material has such a warm luster and takes on life when the light changes. These are dynamic sculptures with amazing renderings, and something I never tire of."

Stephen continues to collect. "At first I decided to stick with men of letters, until I found a bust of David Garrick that I know is an early example of its type. The detail is beautiful, and the modeling crisp. I often buy at auction. And, though the competition isn't huge, there's always someone who bids against me right down to the line." He also accumulates other smaller examples of the neoclassical taste, like intaglios and plaster casts, keeping to a monochrome palette and arranging each object carefully.

The new apartment is designed to show off these collections in fine style, with its fireplace and tall ceilings. "I've gone through lots of phases when it comes to taste," says Stephen, "but this one is with me to stay."

DIANE MARTINSON
NEOCLASSICAL VISION

Eighteenth-century French antique engravings signal Diane Martinson's taste for classical objects, which she uses throughout her house. The designer and her husband are avid collectors of stone sculptures and sepia engravings, which cued the colors she chose. "I kept to a color scheme like old stone—gray and beige and cream—on the table as well as in the room." Even the floor is a smooth wave of light cream. The rich but reticent tones let her set the table as she pleases, here with an assortment of objects and china, with unique Wedgwood pieces among them that bring an imaginary neoclassical space to mind.

OPPOSITE: Candlesticks in Wedgwood's Edme, which was designed in 1908 for the French market as a new shape for creamware, seem like classical columns, replicating others that Diane has placed on her table. Blush roses bring a romantic touch to this neoclassical tablescape.

"I love to think of a theme and bring it to life on the table," Diane says. Well known as an innovative designer/producer of linens and objects for the table, she loves variety on a tabletop. She gave this Valentine's Day table a "'love among the ruins' theme," choosing miniature classical columns and urns, even the pediment from a Roman ruin as a centerpiece, and adding ivory-handled antique cutlery, her mother's ivory napkin rings, and vintage Wedgwood.

Diane is passionate about table appointments, and when she and her husband, Bob, moved from a 6,000-square-foot house to this simple Long Island farmhouse less than half that size, making sure there was room for all the china she's amassed over the years was a priority for her. "Luckily we have a big basement, and we just lined the walls of it with metal shelving." That gave her more than enough room for a lifetime's treasure trove of dishware. She and Bob—who is also enthusiastic about china gathering—rarely miss a sale. "We thinned many of our collections before we moved."

The Wedgwood remained, however. "Wedgwood drabware is my everyday place setting, and food looks so good on it," Diane explains. "Just as we moved I went to a tag sale where there was a boxful under a table, and reasonably priced. But I was stern with myself and walked away—and it still haunts me!" Her husband is just as enthusiastic about the great plate hunt: "We were in Connecticut on a garden tour when we found Wedgwood commemorative plates for the Garden Club of America, with beautiful sepia prints, each one different, on the creamware plates. I said no, but he said, 'Oh! I'm a gardener; we must get them.' And I'm so glad we did—the price of vintage Wedgwood is always on the rise, as people value their quality and style."

For Diane, preparing a pretty table is as important as making sure those plates are filled with delicious food. "People who know me, and that I've spent my whole life working with things for the table, have come to expect something a little different when they sit down. I get pleasure from it, and so do they!"

OPPOSITE: Though their sources are not the same, each of these distinct objects speaks to the other, which attracts the eye.

SUZANNE RHEINSTEIN
A SOUTHERN TRADITION

Magnates and movie stars have Suzanne Rheinstein on their speed dial; not only is she one of their Los Angeles designers of choice, but her generous-hearted entertaining, which combines California ease with her New Orleans–bred unique style, brings much of Hollywood (and those from beyond) to her home for parties that buzz. Between soirees they can visit Suzanne at Hollyhock, her store in West Hollywood, which offers her signature style, with fabrics, furniture, and objects based on a love of the antique, but shot through with California sunshine. At home, a classic 1920s center hall neo-Georgian, her use of good eighteenth-century furniture and a fine assortment

OPPOSITE: Silver and sparkle from the antique Russian chandelier might lend a formal tone, but Suzanne believes nothing is too precious to be used. She sets the table with what she loves, like this eighteenth-century blue Wedgwood covered dish and old creamware. She sees no need to gussy up a place setting with a mat and prefers to see her fine things reflected in the well-polished table.

of eighteenth- and nineteenth-century Wedgwood illustrates her easy way with grand style. "I'm not really a collector; I just buy what I love—and I use it," she says. That means important pieces, like the Swedish side table in the dining room or a cloud bank of pale creamware in the cupboard, are chosen for their look and their patina. Suzanne emphasizes the sensuous appeal of antiques with this play of texture on texture: "I love the feel of old creamware in the hand, the way it just floats; it's so light. And I adore the shapes—so simple, so elegant. I am very drawn to the outline, the silhouette of everything." Creamware was her first love in the Wedgwood lexicon, but she says, "I travel, and I look, and see other things I become interested in. The black basalt has some severity to it, and is a great contrast to the creamware." And the frisking putti and graceful nymphs often found on it are appealing to her good-humored style.

The sun plays on objects throughout the house, striking a spark on some old Sheffield plate, snared by an eighteenth-century Wedgwood black basalt teapot, and caught by a Russian chandelier hung with glass as clear and cascading as raindrops. "I love light in all its manifestations, and I do everything to encourage it in the house," she says. "The walls in the dining room are glazed, the better to reflect the light. I watch the sun change throughout the day, from the bright morning sun to the more dappled light at the end of the day."

For an evening party, all those candles are alight, and guests may be seated at the gleaming mahogany table, or a buffet

OPPOSITE: Suzanne loves the marks of time: If the detailing on the side table is rubbed, it's part of its rich past life; it's fine if the silver loses its plating. The Queensware dishes, originally designed in 1776, live easily in this rich mix.

BELOW: Texture tells the tale, from the engine-engraved lines on the black basalt jug and teapot to the delicate tendrils hand-painted on the eighteenth-century Wedgwood cream plates.

LEFT: A simple pine table is set in the "Back House" by the pool. Suzanne collects handblown glass containers for her candles and scatters them among the Wedgwood plates next to generous linen napkins and amethyst glasses.

BELOW: The hand-painted creamware plate is decorated with a design including grape leaves and grapes, a popular motif in the 1800s, with its reminder of the joys of wine.

OPPOSITE, LEFT: The two magnificent Wedgwood bulb pots that center the table are decorated with acanthus leaves, a motif in use for two thousand years. Deep brown glaze and gilding mean these were expensive pieces when they were first made in the early nineteenth century.

encourages them to float through the house and settle anywhere from garden to living room. "I buy Sheffield plate as well as sterling, because I love the slightly worn effect, especially in candlelight, when it adds to the shimmer," Suzanne explains. She uses many antiques—"painted furniture, quirky things"— at home and in her clients' houses. "I think it's more interesting, more personal, to live with what you like."

DECORATION

Her menu often draws from her New Orleans roots. "I try for an atmosphere that has formal elements but that's also festive and celebratory. I love to set out huge buffets. Southern food is a surprise for most; I bring out tomato aspic, collard greens, ham biscuits, and shrimp Creole, of course. And we have great music in the background." The key is the air of graciousness and ease on the part of the host and hostess: "We want everyone to relax and be happy. It's a good party when people feel comfortable enough to meet, introduce themselves, and talk all night."

ABOVE RIGHT: The clarity of the design on this early-nineteenth-century beaker shows the translation of old patterns Wedgwood was known for; a Greek key rings the rim, just as it was used as trim in the heyday of the Adam brothers' Georgian architecture.

LORD WEDGWOOD
A FAMILY LEGACY

From the family portraits to the fine examples of Wedgwood china, Lord Wedgwood's house charts history—his is the thirteenth generation since the original family potter, Gilbert Wedgwood, born in 1588. As cozily English as this house appears, in fact Lord Wedgwood and his American wife, Jean, live outside Philadelphia. But their mutual affection for the traditional British way of life and the reminders of Wedgwood's past has prompted them to create a family home that combines American comfort with English style. They were lucky in finding a house with many of the details that gave a suitable backdrop to their life.

OPPOSITE: Designed ten years ago, the Madeleine dinner service is full of neoclassical details. The soft color, the swagged garlands, and the cameo-like picture of a classical maiden bring to mind the art and the architecture of the eighteenth century. Josiah Wedgwood would have marveled at the borders of 22-karat gold—firing gold was a challenge in his time.

ABOVE AND OPPOSITE, BELOW: In the
dining room, warmed with red walls,
the table is set in Wedgwood's
Madeleine. The imposing fireplace is
crowned with a broken pediment
and a broad shelf that allows more
display of fine Wedgwood wares.
The blue and white jasper plaques
were a popular eighteenth-century
way of displaying portraits of the
prominent, while the elaborate
candleholders are reproductions of
neoclassical examples of two
centuries ago.

"And I must say, we collect the things we like and have filled the house," says Lord Wedgwood.

Wedgwood of all periods is, naturally, a favorite feature; however, Lord Wedgwood's pieces come with a special connection: the patina produced by being part of the long family line, with its proud history as the background to every vase and plate.

As a member of Wedgwood's board, and as someone who represents the company and its heritage in many countries, he travels a great deal. When he is at home, the red-walled dining room is one of his favorite places to spend time, especially when there are guests to entertain. "I spend so many hours in airports, and eating in restaurants, that when I am home, I don't want to leave this room," he says. "There's something special about lighting the candles and the oil lamps—we'll light the

ABOVE LEFT: The dining table setting includes napkins with a coronet and glasses from the House of Lords, where Lord Wedgwood served for many years. The orange bowl is an eighteenth-century form made to offer the precious fruits for dessert while showing off their colors.

ABOVE RIGHT: Family silver sparkles, with a tea service and tall candelabra on the sideboard, under the gaze of the ancestors, including an Edwardian grandmother and a Georgian cousin.

ABOVE: Portrait busts were important to the ancient Romans, an enthusiasm that was revived in the eighteenth century, partly from interest in the Roman antiques, but also as a way of celebrating the dignity of man. Josiah Wedgwood saw plaster examples and knew he could do better; in 1773 he began to produce them, mostly, as here, in black basalt, often modeled by his best artists. George Washington, *right,* and Josiah Wedgwood himself, *left,* are among Lord Wedgwood's collection. The Josiah bust dates to 1940.

CENTER LEFT: The broken pediment above the door frames this rare jasper medallion of George Washington. Josiah Wedgwood supported the American Revolution and knew Benjamin Franklin well. He added American luminaries to his extensive list of worthies depicted on medallions and intaglios, from ancients to moderns.

CENTER RIGHT: George Stubbs's portrait of Josiah Wedgwood and his family is the iconic picture of the master of Etruria. This covered jar, complete with figurative finial, was made for the bicentenary of Josiah Wedgwood's death in 1795.

whole first floor with candles—and having a dinner with good wine and good food. In that wonderful glow, I think people relax and start to talk about all the things that are important." A guest could be forgiven for wanting to come back in the daylight to have a good look at the Wedgwoodiana that is on display. Ancestor portraits, fine examples of some of the more unusual Wedgwood creations, and a glittering array of old Waterford are everywhere. "I'm afraid I am a bit of a china-holic," he says with a grin. "Jean and I both are. I enjoy designs of all eras, and have quite a few—we can set the table in many different ways or simply display fine examples, like the Ruby Tonquin on the sideboard; it's such a dynamic and exciting pattern." Its bold Chinese red and gold flower motif was designed in the 1930s.

Other tablewares have a background unique to Lord Wedgwood: The goblets were given to him by friends when he left the House of Lords. He also has many of the most bravura pieces from Wedgwood's current production, revivals of grand eighteenth-century pieces like the perfect-in-every-detail creamware candlesticks on the mantelpiece. He put the black and white footed vase with its gilded representation of his coat of arms "front and center—it's important that people know that our craftsmanship is as impeccable as ever, both in modeling and in firing." And, of course, on display are samples of the Wedgwood factory's earliest productions, like the jasper medallions that eighteenth-century cognoscenti would put in their libraries, including a very rare one of George Washington. "Josiah had great sympathy with the American Revolution, and a great friendship with Benjamin Franklin, too," Lord Wedgwood explains. Franklin's years as ambassador in London brought him into contact with Wedgwood and others who shared his interest in scientific innovation.

Some corners reveal another side to Lord Wedgwood, who was raised in Kenya, where his parents had moved when they fell in love with the country. "Well, we do have sort of an eclectic mix," he admits. That means here and there are faux animal print fabrics or an oil painting of a cheetah.

BELOW: Prowling green Chinese Tigers on the teacups aren't the only animal life in the library; faux fur appears on pillows and the rug. This 1984 china pattern recalls the many revivals of the taste for chinoiserie. In Georgian times, the passion for Chinese objects was fired with the first imports; teapots and teacups were modeled on the Chinese originals.

However farflung his travels, he knows he will come home to the old rituals, including his favorite dinners. He revels in a multicourse meal, working his way through a starter, a roast, a pudding, some cheese, perhaps, and even more important, time spent together by candlelight. "As I travel and talk to people, I am convinced we are discovering again the importance of a proper dinnertime, with nice china and enough leisure to talk. It is the basis of a family, and of a friendship."

MICHAEL SMITH
L.A. STYLE

Early one morning, Michael Smith is on the Eurostar from London to Paris, taking calls and notes as he hurtles through the countryside. He is a busy man, interior designer to the Hollywood firmament and the megamagnates, apt to quote a compliment from Evelyn de Rothschild or be photographed standing in another gracious living room he's designed in one of Tinseltown's iconic houses. His rooms are subtle; the tutored eye notices the fine pieces of Chinese porcelain and the exquisite lines on the tailored curtains, but most of all the artful blend of world-class antiques with imaginative furniture and luxurious details.

OPPOSITE: Shells of all shapes were made in creamware and tinted with a variety of natural shell colors; an Edme dinner plate, designed in the twentieth century, echoes the radiating grooves of the shell. This informal setting derives its quiet elegance from the care with which the table is set: silver on rattan, glass on stone, with a maroon shell centerpiece.

With his own fabrics, furniture, and other home furnishings—the collections named for his dog, Jasper—Michael can command exactly what is necessary for each challenge. He is fluent in many decorating vocabularies, so he is able to create grand and magisterial effects in one house and make room for coziness in another—especially his own.

As effortless as his rooms look, there is diligent thinking and top craftsmanship—and shopping—behind each one. That's why he's on the Eurostar, taking in the cream of the antiques shops in London and Paris, finding treasures for clients—and perhaps for himself. "I've been an antiques hunter since I was very young," he says. "As a boy growing up in California, I'd haunt the antiques shops." It was a lucky find one day that provoked his interest in old Wedgwood. "I was drawn to the beauty of the plate, not just the design, but the

shape, and the way it felt in the hand. It was an eye-opener, and I've continued to collect what I like."

Michael buys these pieces to use at home in Bel Air, where he lives with his two Labradoodles. "I am very fond of the English influence on house design," he says; the Wedgwood china is one example, accompanied by his love of classical proportions mixed with a touch or two of idiosyncrasy. He also believes in the luxury that can be devoted to the basics of everyday living—his shower is Egyptian alabaster, his mattress custom made, and there's a chef in the kitchen—so, of course, if one loves the colors of an early-nineteenth-century plate, bring it out and enjoy it, and share it with friends. "It's the things you surround yourself with, that you touch every day, that make a big difference in your life."

ABOVE: After dinner, in the library, Michael brings out a fine early-nineteenth-century Wedgwood dessert set with coffee. The understated decor is about texture as much as color. The dessert set comes into its own; the broad, deep green border, *left,* is decorated with budding twigs and a twist of flowers. The serving dishes, *right,* would have held cakes or fruit.

BARDITH
COLLECTORS' PARADISE

On Manhattan's Madison Avenue, one store window has halted connoisseurs of antique tableware in their tracks for forty-five years. With its unmistakable displays crowded with impeccable pieces of china in every shape, Bardith is the magnet for those who love pottery and porcelain produced in eighteenth- and early-nineteenth-century France, China, Holland, and England. Fine examples of Wedgwood, a specialty of the shop, are prominent among them, along with creamware and painted porcelain from other prominent factories in England and Europe like Spode and Meissen. The dignity of the forms lends the shop a quiet air, even as every surface is full of the sorts of high-style examples that the collectors covet.

OPPOSITE: A pair of 1800–1810 tureens in cream-colored earthenware. Based on a glacier, the shape held ice cream but was probably intended for plain cream as part of a dessert service.

It is dazzling—here a biscuit jar, there a candlestick, rows of plates arranged by color and design, a grand tureen. Everything is crowded, yet ordered, resulting in towers of irreplaceable objects that make a visitor walk gently while seeing the best examples of pottery and porcelain made in the eighteenth and early nineteenth centuries. On display are the development and fashions of grand tableware, the history of china over several centuries.

"Every time period has its own favorite, and taste runs in cycles. The neoclassical taste that brought Josiah Wedgwood success is popular again today," says Steve Wolf, who owns the store with his mother, Edith. He points out the neoclassically inspired tureens and vases on every side. "The spare and evocative designs jibe with our modern sense of simplicity. Look at these eighteenth-century Wedgwood creamware tureens: The design is in perfect proportion without an extra line."

Collectors come to serve their own passions; some are very specific—eighteenth-century armorial creamware, for instance. And as with every precious object, scarcity affects value. It is surprising that so much survived merry Georgian dining or life on a Victorian mantelpiece; certainly those without a nick or a crack are the most valued. Other customers come for a grand piece that will make a room or a table; setting the places with contemporary creamware, perhaps, and buying candlesticks or a tureen for a point of beauty.

"Josiah Wedgwood was a genius," Steve says, citing Wedgwood's drive for experiment. "So many copied him—and the imitators would copy a signature, too—watch out for 'Vedgwood' and 'Wedgewood' with an 'e.' Other factories brought out their own versions of what Wedgwood had made so successful. And Wedgwood has used some designs for two hundred fifty years; there is a very reliable dating method, however, in the marks on the base."

OPPOSITE: These shapes show the wide range of Wedgwood style at the beginning of the nineteenth century; many had been in use for fifty years—and even today might inspire a Wedgwood line. *Top:* The soup plate with leaf and nut border is white ware and dates from 1810 to 1820. *Center left:* A cream-colored earthenware tureen has been painted with a blue and gold laurel border. *Center right:* The earliest pieces here are four cream-colored earthenware plates with a pierced border and a shell edge. Work like this demanded skilled artisans. *Bottom:* A herring at the bottom of this 1820–1830 dish signaled its contents—this piece was made for the Dutch market, where herring was a staple.

Experience, too, teaches one how to evaluate a piece; eighteenth-century Wedgwood creamware, for instance, is much lighter in the hand than later editions. "Try to handle and see as much of the real Wedgwood as you can. And, though you can imitate Wedgwood designs, imitating the craftsmanship is very difficult. My mother always cautioned me that when I looked at a piece with applied figures of classical themes, I should look at the feet of the putti. If they stand on the line as if they are weight bearing, and are crisply cut, the piece is probably fine. If they are floating in space—that's a bad sign."

Each piece at Bardith speaks to the collector who likes the history, the stories, as well as the aesthetics. "I like the simplicity of the black basalt pieces," says Steve Wolf, and he adds a story. "Wedgwood wrote his partner Bentley twenty years after its invention to say people still couldn't get enough of it, because hostesses loved the way the black background made their hands appear even whiter." With this small detail he brings back the dinner parties and the tea tables, and the long-ago hostesses who would set their table with such prizes, adjusting a plate here, a vase there, bringing beauty to the table with every touch.

JOHN PAWSON
DESIGN FOR LIVING

*I*n England, a country that once deemed a house underdressed if it didn't boast two layers of curtains and carpeting on every floor, the architect John Pawson attracted immediate notice when he finished his own family's home in 1999. A Victorian terraced cottage in west London, its period facade remained intact—but inside, every bit of ornament had disappeared, as had much of the back wall, which was replaced by glass. Light bathed a kitchen/dining room that was a creamy expanse of limestone on floor and counter; almost all was hidden in white cupboards. An immediate talking point, the house was John's declaration of the appropriateness of minimalism at home. When people asked, "How can you live like that?"

OPPOSITE: Synonymous with clear-cut, frill-free modern design, the British architect John Pawson sets his table with Queensware, drawn by its shape as well as its practicality. He deems it harmonious and unobtrusive, affording the pleasure of food and conversation free play. On the table, he's partnered the pottery with perfectly balanced eighteenth-century cutlery, the knife with a pistol handle.

LEFT: The designer in him admires the plates' perfectly planned concave rim that keeps food in place; the bowls' origins lie in the ancient Chinese tea bowl. Pawson is drawn to the truly refined, with nothing extraneous.

CENTER: Braised endive, in a flat soup plate, carefully and simply prepared, waits for dinner.

OPPOSITE: Stacks of Queensware and rows of unadorned glasses are stored in the cupboard.

he countered, "This is how I live, so this is what my house needs to be like."

It seemed the logical end point to the modernists' urge to simplify, simplify. It's not about absence, he would say, but about appropriateness. There's nothing spartan about his life. The kitchen, which leads onto the garden, is the scene for gatherings large and small, whether on a night when a fire burns in the mantel-less fireplace, or on a summer day when diners wander between garden and table.

This twenty-first-century architect serves his meals using one of Wedgwood's oldest patterns, Queensware, which also suited Queen Charlotte in the eighteenth century. Nearly everything he and his family have chosen "finds its roots in the

past. Contrary to the belief that modern equates with futuristic, our choice of china is the traditional Wedgwood Queensware. It appears undesigned compared to most contemporary dinnerware." It's "unselfconscious," he adds, and he approves of its practical nature, too, the creamy background to allow food to show off its color, and the design of the pieces that, like his house, are about a clean silhouette and working efficiently.

Such simplicity yields a rich experience. As Pawson explains, "The result of all this—we hope—is one of harmony, where there is nothing to distract from the food and the wine, and the vital process of enjoying yourself."

TRICIA FOLEY
WINTER WHITE GATHERING

Visit Tricia Foley on the Upper East Side of Manhattan, and you'll walk down an avenue where city life fills the air. There are people everywhere, shopping or walking toward Central Park, and the subway growls beneath the pavement. But open the door to Tricia's apartment, and the hustle and noise disappear in the light-filled space of her 1874 brownstone. Here, the old mahogany paneling reflects the light, and all is calm and orderly. Files are tucked neatly in overscale silver punch bowls, and flowering white quince branches are in a glass cylinder near Tricia as she works at the big antique table, some Mozart playing in the background.

OPPOSITE: Tricia can, as she did here, plan a party in a moment—on a snowy Sunday in New York, she invited friends in for a celebration, with the fireplace as the focal point of this winter white party. She depends on her collection of china; the classic shapes of vintage and modern Wedgwood black basalt plates and vases are something to be savored against the natural linen.

"I need a refuge," she says. Luggage flanks the front door, a sign that she's off on another trip soon. "I work with color and pattern all the time, and I need a calm environment in which to do that," she says. The space, decorated in whites and natural linens, offers a respite from all the color in Tricia's professional life.

She's worked on all sorts of home design projects as an editor, an interior designer, a product developer, or a producer of advertisements, catalogs, and iconic style books. Most recently, she was president of Wedgwood USA. "The first time I visited Barlaston I was overwhelmed by being where this historic china is made, seeing the old potteries around me, watching the artisans make a plate with all the skills and attention of those eighteenth-century workers. I was fortunate enough to go into the archives, where the original molds are stored, and see Josiah Wedgwood's experiment books and the pattern books—a real source of inspiration."

Her own history has its Wedgwood roots. As the oldest of seven children, Tricia often went to her grandparents' house nearby; her English grandmother made sure the kettle was on and let her choose a favorite cup from her collection—often a Wedgwood cup. That shared time, and tea, became intertwined with feelings of comfort and coziness. "We were always drinking tea in my family—for celebration, for consolation, for companionship."

As she grew up, and her taste evolved, she became more drawn to the simplest of designs and silhouettes. "It started when I studied at Parsons, which was loyal to the Bauhaus ideals of simplicity." Creamware old and new became her passion; now she'll float through the crush of Portobello market and spot an eighteenth-century teacup and saucer among the crowds. Tricia's hidden cupboards are filled with dozens of

OPPOSITE: Flowering quince branches and large silver punch bowls set the scene for the bar setup. Everything does double duty in Tricia's household—the bowls make good ice buckets. Tricia is known for her disciplined tastes and inspired eye, which is why she's drawn to pieces of the simplest, and most perfect, design, her narrow palette a way to emphasize the purity of their shape and proportion.

pieces—she especially loves Queensware and Jasper Conran's mugs, as well as glasses, bowls, and vases. I do have service for twenty-four in many patterns . . . just as much as I treasure those sets, I also have single samples I've collected over the years. Everything is put to work around here." She uses what she buys for photo shoots. A cup or plate discovered years ago in a London shop might show up on the Wedgwood Web site, in a magazine story, in a Ralph Lauren ad, or in the pages of one of her books.

Because Tricia is known to entertain with an hour's notice, she'll take the files out of the bowls, clear the table, put the flowers in a favorite vase, and arrange linen napkins on the table. Candles here and there add their warm glow, while the platters of food are as carefully displayed as those flowering branches in the vases.

With twenty-five in her immediate family, she is used to serving multitudes. "I love to see friends, and sometimes an impromptu dinner, with take-out Indian curries decanted into antique creamware bowls, is a way to get us together, informally, but with a sense of occasion," she says. "Other times, like a winter Sunday last year, with a surprise snowstorm, I thought—let's have a party." And two hours later, she did.

JAMES HUNIFORD
DOWNTOWN SETTING

The table is set for supper in the kitchen, the door open to the garden, the setting sun serene. Interior designer James "Ford" Huniford is folding napkins when his two-year-old son appears, careering on his tricycle around the slender stand holding an eighteenth-century tureen. Ford turns Jack gently, and the boy happily scrambles off down the hall. "I want to make sure my children are comfortable here," he says, unperturbed. His infant daughter has yet to explore her surroundings, but Ford has anticipated the future. His sculpture by Donald Judd that hangs above the kitchen's cream-colored banquette ("it's scrubbable") is now boxed protectively in Lucite, and antique tureens are used just for special occasions.

OPPOSITE: Ford layers his table as he does his rooms. A Swedish pottery bowl tops two Wedgwood plates: At the bottom are some vintage drabware, in its characteristic khaki tone, and a creamware plate in a cauliflower pattern.

ABOVE LEFT: The cauliflower plate had its origins in the potters' magic of the mid-eighteenth century, when teapots in a harvest of vegetable shapes were hugely popular.

ABOVE RIGHT: A plant stand shaped like an eccentric branch holds an eighteenth-century creamware Wedgwood tureen that is simply edged with a thin brown line and filled with ranunculus.

OPPOSITE AND FOLLOWING PAGES: Low cowhide stools and a sleek cream banquette create the perfect setting for this summer supper, mixing antique and new Wedgwood collections.

Ford is a partner in the renowned design firm Sills Huniford, which has been a much-praised interior design company for more than twenty years. The firm's style draws on four centuries of Italian, Belgian, Austrian, and French antiques, impeccable architecture, a bit of whimsy, and a feeling for luxury, using materials like shagreen and parchment. They create an atmosphere that is at once exciting but peaceful, traditional in its elements but thoroughly modern in its approach.

His own house carries on the theme. A decorator, a modernist, and a classicist, Ford makes the most of every era, his refined taste tying it all together. Here in the kitchen, cream and brown are the background to an assortment of furniture and objects that catch the eye, yet are not so obtrusive that they dominate. "I mix it up," says Ford. "I want my home to be calming and soothing." Friends and family know he is a spontaneous and excellent host, ready to pull out the campaign table, built for soldiers' travel with drop leaves and drawers for equipment, and choose from his Wedgwood vintage pieces.

Wedgwood suits him, not as an antiques collector, but because old pieces deliver just what he's after: quirkiness, texture, another note in the mix.

"I was drawn at first to the color of some plates I found, so simple, with this wonderful muddy tone," he explains. The plates were drabware, and are still favorites for their versatility and quiet presence on the table. "I like to discover things wherever I travel. I'm always poking in flea markets and thrift shops." Gradually Ford built up more of his drabware collection, as well as more Wedgwood in black and white. "And I don't buy for the closet. I use everything, however precious. I have lots of cupboards; I don't like china on display."

With a squeal of wheels, the little boy returns for another lap of the kitchen, before Ford shoos him back down the hallway, and serenity is restored once more.

THE OUTSTANDING DESIGNERS OF TODAY,
WHETHER ACTIVE IN THE FIELDS OF INTERIORS
OR FASHION, ARE EXCITED BY THE OPPORTUNITY
TO MATCH THEIR TALENTS TO THE WEDGWOOD
TRADITION. JASPER CONRAN, VERA WANG,
BARBARA BARRY, AND MARTHA STEWART ARE
AMONG THOSE WHO HAVE PRODUCED POPULAR
LINES FOR WEDGWOOD, ENABLING EVERYONE TO
HAVE HIGH STYLE ON THE TABLE.

DESIGNED FOR TODAY

JASPER CONRAN
ENGLISH STYLE

ew people get to inhabit a dream. And yet British designer Jasper Conran has managed to do just that. But then, his creativity, like his dream, has few bounds. "I wanted a Queen Anne house in the country. One that no one had 'improved'; I wanted a moldy old kitchen and peeling paint. After looking in the country, and finding nothing, I went to the old London suburb of Chiswick— and there it was, Walpole House. Untouched, after ninety years of residence by the same family." The Thames flows in front, and there are gardens with fragrant old magnolia trees that scent the air each April and a redbrick building with its Tudor chimneys and later Gothic details.

OPPOSITE: Jasper often invites friends for dinner at the long table in the dining room. His own design Platinum Stripe dinner service, his cutlery, and his Shine glassware pick up the gleam of the fireplace as do the fine Georgian silver candlesticks.

ABOVE: Pale gray paneling is the backdrop to this gilded side table, where Platinum espresso cups wait beneath an Elizabethan portrait.

OPPOSITE, BELOW LEFT: The perfect Elizabethan chairs stand to the side, under a Venetian mirror with more silvery glow. Jasper has collected dozens of napkins at antiques fairs—all are embroidered with his initials.

OPPOSITE, BELOW RIGHT: A plate in Platinum can be mixed with other elements to add interest to the table. The silvery sheen is reflected in the baroque silver sauce jug and the saltcellar with its little shovel. Saltcellars have often been fanciful in design; this one resembles a dairy bucket. With all the decoration on the table, Jasper likes flowers in simple glass vases.

"At first, we had to fix the dangerous things, like ancient wiring. Then, it was more conservation than restoration. It's always a narrow line—you don't want to destroy what's wonderful by overworking it." His own deep knowledge of the period, coupled with his sense of design, was brought into play. Finally, each corner was brought to life again, with Jasper's collection of paintings from the first hundred years of English art, 1550–1660, on the historically accurate painted walls and impeccably sourced period furniture in place.

Jasper likes the house to be filled with friends, especially for dinners of many courses, served properly, in the dining room. At these "jolly good parties" the room is lit by candles, with the crackle of the fire as background music, and the table is set with "a judicious mix of old and new": his own design china next to a Georgian silver sauceboat ("I have a thing for sauceboats").

Throughout the house are examples of tableware Jasper has designed for Wedgwood for the last decade. Jasper trained in England and America, and found almost instant success as a fashion designer. Now he puts his mark on everything from stage productions to housewares. "When Wedgwood asked me to work with them, I was *thrilled.* I knew their history, and their quality." His first formal service, snow white bone china called Jasper Conran White, has been a hit since 2001. He has added others that mix and match or stand on their own, including an informal creamy earthenware, Jasper Conran Casual, that was an instant classic. Though he toured the archives, he was interested in designing his own shapes, with a distinctive sharply cut handle that makes his wares immediately recognizable.

Jasper is a man who lives with objects of the past, but he is

BELOW: The small dining room recalls the Regency rage for chinoiserie, prompted by the Prince Regent's Pavilion at Brighton filled with rich colors and "Chinese" details. This hand-painted wallpaper in a saturated green is full of flowers, as is Jasper's design for Chinoiserie Green, which can be mixed with Chinoiserie White and others in his line, or to add some spark to a pure white china place setting. His own design green leather mats are added to his table; tulips are in a vase from his Waterford crystal collection.

not imprisoned by them. He calls his design process "extrapolation" as well as inspiration. "I saw an incredibly elegant jug, for instance, and went off to draw it. When I compared the drawing and the original, they were nothing alike—I had transformed it without realizing it." Jasper's goal is to incorporate "what I feel about the past, a sense of 'Englishness' without being ersatz." That means evolving a piece to freshen it, yet not too much. He always leaves something that chimes with the buyer: for the blue and white Blue Butterfly collection, there is no historical document at its root, but memories of old English delftware, and the centuries' love of the blue and white combination. His Chinoiserie pattern was designed "because I love the history of Chinese taste in English design; in the eighteenth century anyone who was anyone had a room with Chinese wallpaper." This design, too, is a respectful nod to the originals, with a more freehand simplification of its birds and vines motif.

Walpole House remains a place that delights him, where his own creations sit serenely among the historically correct, a sort of dialogue between yesterday and today. "The house tells you what it wants, and tells you what it doesn't want," he says, as he bars yellow roses from its flower vases.

The house, these days, must be quite content. And so is Jasper, especially when he wakes on a sunny day and sees the light reflected from the river flowing outside, flickering and flashing as it has for centuries.

VERA WANG
NEW YORK BRIDAL SHOWER

The name Vera Wang is synonymous with weddings. Her thoroughly contemporary yet romantic take on the day has defined our era's understanding of one of life's most extraordinary rituals. She's also translated her style for Wedgwood, with hope chests and bridal lists in mind, producing the kind of tableware that tempts brides to carry a picture in their minds of dinner à deux by candlelight—after all, doesn't a circlet of gold around a plate remind her of a wedding band?

OPPOSITE: Gilded Leaf plates, with their delicate vine threaded around the rim, are matched with champagne flutes in Leaf. Gilded Weave plates, with a wider border like a gold mesh ribbon, are added to the mix.

When one of Vera's assistants announced her engagement, Vera's loft-showroom in the garment district in mid-Manhattan became just the place for her colleagues to throw a surprise shower for her. The utilitarian space is filled with sumptuous gowns hanging all around, looking as if they are about to be asked to dance. Outside, the bounce and blare of traffic rules and carts trundle bolts of fabric, but inside, a long table has been prepared for the bride-to-be's arrival, her friends full of cheer as they pile the presents high. In a moment, here comes the bride—and everyone clinks a champagne glass or two.

Lunch is served on some of Vera's discreetly lavish designs for Wedgwood, which were themselves inspired by her wedding dress

ABOVE: The dessert plate that can, perhaps, hold the groom's cake for next year's anniversary celebration contrasts with the Gilded Leaf plates. The delicate vine that spirals to the center has small leaves that change from platinum to gold along the way—perhaps a reminder to any bride that wedded life may bring change but always remains precious.

OPPOSITE, ABOVE AND BELOW LEFT: A big bouquet of Vera's signature flower, the calla lily, in creamy white, has its own stately presence on the buffet table.

OPPOSITE, ABOVE RIGHT: The Gilded Weave pattern rings the bottom of the cup, which is in Wedgwood's traditional "can" shape—straight-sided coffee cups were called "cans" in the eighteenth century.

OPPOSITE, BELOW RIGHT: Vera's Trellis silver flatware is like the silver designs that were once an important part of a bride's dowry. Though the decoration is ornate and rich, the trellis that gives it its name is apparent, especially when the table is set in the French manner, with the silver forks placed tines down.

designs. The understated yet opulently produced china, with its touches of platinum and gold, and her silver and glass are the choice of many couples. Each comes with a promise—as the years grow, so can the collection, as new designs are added that mix happily with the old.

The table is a study in contrasts, and full of surprises; the tablecloths, for instance, are simply pieces of natural linens, organdies, and silks in different weights, layered for an informal and relaxed feel. The bride-to-be toasts her friends with a smile—and then it's back to work, to make another bride's dream come true.

BARBARA BARRY
GRACIOUS ENTERTAINING

I'm running to the farmers' market. The Gaviota straw-berries are in—Heaven!" says designer Barbara Barry, on the way out of her Beverly Hills door. In just a little while, friends will arrive at her home with its sweeping staircase and lavish gardens, and all will be ready for an informal fill-your-plate lunch. The table is set with Boxwood and Topiary china she designed for Wedgwood that was inspired by her own garden, while the abundance of fine cheese, crusty bread, and fresh salads are the luxuries Californians enjoy. With the doors open to the terrace, there's also plenty of California sunlight.

OPPOSITE: The first collection Barbara made for Wedgwood was Curtain Call: The black scallops around the gilded rim are a reminder of a looped stage curtain. A snappy contrast comes with the very graphic new lily plate. Versatility reigns—the silver flagon does duty as a sugar bowl, along with a cream jug that recalls Georgian originals.

"I love this house," she enthuses. "It encompasses all the good things about Los Angeles: greenery, fragrant smells of orange blossom and jasmine, privacy, a little hideaway. I travel the world and then come back and get my work done."

A homecoming is also the time for entertaining in a style she calls "informal but special. Even if I don't have time to entertain, I fantasize about it a lot! I want people to feel comfortable and pampered. I know how to live well, and I realized it doesn't take a lot of stuff, but good, simple, and honest things, like a

ABOVE AND RIGHT: A casual meal by the pool, set out so family and friends can come when they please and fill a plate with cheese and bread and salad, is surrounded by the cool green of Barbara's garden. Her love of boxwood is borne out by the china in Topiary and Maze patterns, with a refined topknot of topiary on one and green hedges on the other. She experiments with her new designs at her own table—and small tabletop topiaries complete the theme.

little round breadboard from my favorite London store, with a hunk of beautiful bread on it, and English butter and Armenian apricot jam in one of my own gray pots I threw as a beginner, or a cup of the hottest coffee with steaming milk and a huge linen throw on your lap. All these details make people feel loved—and that's what it's all about."

Barbara Barry has created china, silver, and glass for Wedgwood, an outgrowth of her career as a successful interior designer with an art school background. When she began to design for Wedgwood "I went *crazy* in the archives, especially those from the eighteenth century—the designs were so surprisingly modern and pared down. I love how Josiah always worked with the talent of the day and I feel honored to be part of that legacy. I was able to pull from various collections and put together shapes that traditionally don't go together."

Barbara draws from her own love of the table and easy entertaining. "Nature has been my highest inspiration, the elegant patterns and the delicious colorations that are found in the natural world." For her Radiance, she was inspired by the sea anemone, with its radiating dots and starlike patterning.

OPPOSITE, ABOVE LEFT: Barbara collects linens and silver; open a drawer and find an assortment of napkin rings. In another, place cards are ready.

OPPOSITE, ABOVE RIGHT: The designs depend on the contrast of gold and white: The plates in the Radiance pattern mix little golden dots, radiating like bursts of fireworks.

OPPOSITE, BELOW LEFT: Each table Barbara sets draws on her treasures, used in new ways according to mood or occasion.

OPPOSITE, BELOW RIGHT: Curtain Call crystal is set out for a welcoming drink, with a silver cup pressed into service as a nut dish.

ABOVE: On a spring day, the green of the garden counterpoints the table's collection of champagne-colored china.

Other patterns draw on lilies or those boxwood topiaries that appear in her own garden. She adores inventing at the table, so she makes designs that mix and match; anyone can give a little shake-up to a familiar setting with the addition of a figured plate or two.

An empty table is as inviting as a pristine scrapbook page; setting it gives her great pleasure. This easy layering makes a table as infinitely variable as a well-chosen wardrobe, with the added scope for creative flourishes. "I love the way a table feels like a blank canvas. It reflects the mood you are in, the entertaining you are doing, the flowers and the food of the season." She keeps cupboards of things to ring changes on a setting. "I have picked up 'little bits' since I was a teen! I love the little things one sees at close range while dining, like a place card. All my work is about 'relatedness' and how things speak to each other. The pairing of the old and the new is always thrilling, like long lost relatives who come to meet in another century. If you choose simple forms and subtle pattern you will find you can create a wardrobe of objects that go together seamlessly. I was always searching for products that have a warm modernity to them, and a certain simple elegance. That makes them fit in seamlessly with all the other beloved objects I already own."

Since her earliest days, Barbara has had a notebook and a pen in her hands, conducting a running reflection of what is around her. Inspiration comes around every corner: "If I hold still long enough, I find something to inspire me and jot it down." For her, design is not just a choice of shape and color but also a reflection of the emotions we bring to our tables. From earliest days, eating together has been part of the bond of humankind, with rituals that reinforce this connection— candlelight or conversation, for instance. "I always say to brides, pick something that feels special, yet is easy to live with. Don't

save all these beautiful things up for guests, but live every day elegantly and fully. Life is so magical, and to tune in to the magic of the every day is what it's all about. You collect memories as well as china, and you layer your life."

When Barbara returns, her arms are laden with strawberries, and soon they are arranged in the perfect bowl. Guests will notice the first of the Gaviotas as they relax in the garden, with the fragrance of the boxwood filling the air, and Barbara will be satisfied and happy. "The home is my muse, and my work has centered around the daily acts of living," she says.

MARTHA STEWART
THE PERFECT SETTING

When Martha Stewart moved to Connecticut in the
1970s, she soon discovered the alluring thrift shops on
the Post Road. With her period house at Turkey Hill
to furnish, and propelled by her lifelong curiosity and
energy, she began to visit these shops. She put her eye
for good design and her constant urge to educate
herself to good use, finding the treasures—such as
eighteenth-century Wedgwood—among the
old chairs and jam jars, carrying them off,
then researching what she'd found, which
sparked a whole new interest. As a fine cook
and entertainer, she used what she bought,
giving that perfect cake an extra boost

OPPOSITE: Martha Stewart's inimit-
able eye for what's beautiful finds its
object everywhere—in the barely-
blue tint of a hen's egg, in a vintage
plate with a twist of gold rim. For
years, she's been leading her public
to these same discoveries—and
compiling her inspiration into new
creations. Flourish, her bone china
pattern for Wedgwood, has an
old-fashioned charm, sweet but not
sugary. The inspiration for this china
service came from a vintage plate
that was refined, its shape
simplified. Its complement is her
new flatware design called Canto.

135

with the consummate cake stand, or filling shelves with the handsomest plates. In her books and magazines she shares this knowledge with readers, not just showing a blue dish but explaining why it was blue, and how it was made.

She loves Wedgwood of all eras, and when she wanted to develop a line of fine tablewares she linked up with the company to produce china, silver, and glass. For inspiration, she turns to her treasure trove, selects favorite examples, and then redesigns them to create new collections with the grace and charm of the old that reflect today's interest in elegant simplicity. The patterns all relate and can be combined with the old and the new for contemporary entertaining. To a palette of white, ecru, gold, and platinum, she adds high notes of color, including one design tinted in her signature robin's egg blue, creating tableware that speaks to both the past and the future by one of the most dedicated of china connoisseurs.

ABOVE LEFT: The gentle blue of the rim comes from Martha's appreciation of natural colors—in this case, the pale blue of birds' eggs.

ABOVE RIGHT: Every day is a celebration with these crystal flutes called Ringlet from Martha Stewart's glassware collection; an etched oval design rings the edge of the glass. A vintage silver tray is the perfect backdrop.

OPPOSITE: A summer evening on a white painted porch, and the table is laid with Martha Stewart's bone china in Flourish with its platinum twining vines, leaves, and berries.

TIMELESS TRADITIONS

WHEN A WEDGWOOD ARTISAN BEGINS WORK, A RICH HISTORY AND DYNAMIC PRESENT ARE IN THE MIX. NOT ONLY ARE THE SHAPES AND COLORS OFTEN THOSE JOSIAH WEDGWOOD KNEW, BUT THE FRESHEST DESIGNS ARE STILL MADE THE OLD WAY—WORKBENCHES HOLD THE OLD MOLDS, AND DESIGNERS PORE OVER THE PATTERN BOOKS. THERE IS A WEALTH OF NEW CHINA SERVICES TO CHOOSE FROM—WITH NEW THEMES AND PATTERN VARIATIONS FROM THE COMPANY'S RICH PAST, COUPLED WITH THE TASTES OF TODAY. THE FOLLOWING PAGES REPRESENT A SAMPLING OF THE CURRENT DESIGNS.

WEDGWOOD WHITES

THE MODERNS

ETERNITY

Thoroughly contemporary-minded china connoisseurs are drawn to Eternity, which has a purity of form and multiplicity of function that reflects the way many of us live today. With a cupboard full of these simple shapes, everything is possible. Like a little black dress, it can be made glamorous or casual, used for whatever is being served: noodles or well-made broth or a towering fruit and ice cream concoction. Unlike the Victorian or Georgian idea of dozens of dishes, each with its own purpose, the Eternity collection has no set ideas: Each perfect white plate or deep bowl displays whatever it contains beautifully. Josiah Wedgwood originally divided his production into useful and ornamental wares, and Eternity china is decidedly useful, a combination of beauty and adaptability.

ROY HARDIN
ARCHITECTS ENTERTAIN

An invitation from Roy Hardin is impossible to resist. His handsome New York loft, which he and his partner, architect Douglas Moss, designed, is the background to their signature easygoing entertaining. "I'm from New Orleans," says Roy. "If there are two people there, it's a party." The loft was designed for comfort and for welcome—there's even a porthole-like opening into the kitchen so the cook, usually Roy, can pass through a plate of fresh oysters and commune with the party even when he's knee-deep in gumbo. "I love cooking at home, and I've been cooking all my life. Whatever the idea of the moment—Cuban, Italian—I'm all over it."

As Fashion Director of Macy's Home Store, he's placed to pick the perfect appointments for his own parties—he sees everything in the market. "The groundbreaking and the staid, the new and the old. I'm exposed to so much. But I know what's important to me, and what will make it happen. When I saw Jasper Conran's china, I knew it would work really well, whether we had a duo or a dozen for dinner.

"I think it is timeless, a new classic that will never date. I like the 'architectural modern' style. And all the pieces—like lots of pitchers of various sizes. It fits the way I like to entertain, putting out platters and bowls of food and jugs with sauces and having each person help himself, and fill and refill his plate." The undecorated but perfectly shaped plates are "just right for a beautiful display of the food, which is part of the fun."

Working with leading Italian designers has given Roy an enthusiasm for their refined take on homewares, and examples of their work are displayed in the loft. Aldo Rossi is a favorite, and his square American cherrywood table, all smooth finish and great solid legs, is the dining table, or the place to put out the dishes for one of their big buffets.

RIGHT: "We like the mixture of pure line with interesting textures in the apartment," says Roy; this Aldo Rossi dining table is the perfect backdrop to carved wooden bowls, pure white of the Jasper Conran plates, and Gio Ponti flatware.

SYLVIA WEINSTOCK
A PIECE OF CAKE

For thirty years, brides have been coming to see Sylvia, whose confiding manner and common sense make her the best companion for any tremulous bride. She was a schoolteacher until her creations were noticed by a top New York caterer—and word of very pleased mouth drew in more clients. She believes in the basics—cakes that taste good, iced in a refined version of buttercream frosting—and she still finds happiness in helping a bride realize her dreams.

Every detail is customized. A bride and her advisers—mother, groom, best friend—come to the Tribeca loft and Sylvia questions them closely about the type of wedding, where it's being held, every detail. They'll settle down with some hot coffee or tea. Then they start a tasting session. Sylvia uses a signature porcelain palette-shaped plate laden with samples of frosting, filling, and cake for them to sample. Hazelnut cake with dark chocolate filling? Carrot cake? Lemon mousse in the middle, or Italian cherries? Which of the three chocolates?

In her atelier she perfects each cake with her talented staff, then transports it to the ceremony—an art in itself, as many of these cakes are ceiling-scrapers. One cake was flown out to serve two thousand of Saudi Arabia's royal family, and Donald Trump's cake for his Plaza wedding was a monument to sumptuousness, but Sylvia is just as interested in the bride whose ideas are of a smaller scale. In fact, she advises that no one overspend on a wedding; she's generous with tips for making the most of the occasion, even if the cake is modest—in her new book, she shares directions for making a simple sugar flower and some arabesques of icing for the do-it-yourselfer.

It pleases her when a bride shares ideas of flowers that mean something special to her, like the roses a grandmother grew, or the freesia her fiancé once gave her, or even a picture of a Dutch still life. Ten women work on the sugar-paste flowers, which are stored in the freezer until use. The flowers, complete from stamen to thorn, are extraordinary. "Preserve them and show some off in a cup or a vase afterward," she advises, as she arranges a small sugar posy in a Wedgwood Eternity cup, for a new lucky bride.

"It's a day about two families, and a love story," she says.

An Eternity teaset complements a white porcelain palette filled with samplings of various cakes, fillings, and frostings. A bride can combine a bit of each till she finds the perfect cake.

THE NATURALS

NATURE
A contemporary expression of nature's design scheme, this pattern, *right*, is inspired by specimens from Josiah Wedgwood's eighteenth-century fossil collection.

ETHEREAL
This thoroughly modern design, *below*, draws on nature. A pattern may be inspired by the breath of wind on water, or a leaf's structure.

NANTUCKET BASKET

Nantucket has long loved that local art and craft—the Nantucket lightship basket. From the early nineteenth century, lightships were manned by crews who wove useful baskets in their spare time. Designer George Davis came to Wedgwood in 1982 with the idea of china based on the baskets, an inspired translation.

PETAL

The English love of countryside is
translated into this appealing white
tea set that incorporates the leaves
and a profusion of petals of a newly
gathered bouquet. The three-
dimensional flowers on Petal raise
these two services almost to the
pleasure of sculpture.

THE CLASSICS

EDME

Edme dates to 1908, when Wedgwood design director John Goodwin was commissioned by French architects and designers Dannier Frères to produce a new design—the ribbed pattern on the edge is an acknowledgment of its architectural origins.

NIGHT AND DAY

In an old-fashioned plate rack, *right*, a wall of texture is created from a sampling of Day white pieces from the the Night and Day collection. Day, made of fine white bone china, uses traditional designs in whole new ways, with textural variations—a checkerboard effect, fluting—on different pieces. Night is an array of coordinating elements in black jasper with glazed interiors. The techniques to produce this variety hark back to Josiah Wedgwood himself, who invented machine turning in 1767 to give a good line to decoration of clay. The pitcher and sugar bowl illustrate fluting, while the large plate at top is covered in checkerboard embossing. Hailed as a twenty-first-century classic, the service was named an Icon of Style by the British Design Council in 2000.

COUNTRYWARE

Simple and elegant, the Countryware pattern, *opposite*, uses a pure white earthenware as the basis for its evocation of the countryside. A raised leaf design circles the plate.

A COUNTRY TABLE
THE NORTH FORK TABLE & INN

When Claudia Fleming, a well-known Manhattan pastry chef, and her husband, chef Gerry Hayden, thought about leaving the city, their thoughts turned to the North Fork, where they had a well-loved second home. They wanted their own restaurant, and more and more they considered venturing to Long Island. "After twenty-five years it was time. We noticed that the North Fork's wineries were producing really good wines, and that there was still farmland, so we could be close to our source of food."

Gerry haunted the real estate agencies, and one day he called Claudia with news about an old inn that had been a community fixture for more than a century. "We bought it, and then knew we had a fix-it-up project on our hands," Claudia explains. Friends and family rallied 'round. Now the old interior of the North Fork Table & Inn has been reinterpreted for today with wainscoting painted taupe, ice blue walls, and natural linens; upstairs, overnight guests find peace and a view over the fields.

When the time came for setting the tables, Claudia chose bone china from Wedgwood's hotel collection, which is the chef's choice for food presentation. Big plates like these allow her room for perfect placement of each element of dessert, "and we needed clean, simple lines and durability," Claudia says. Oversize plates frame the presentation. As the menu works its way through the seasons, its cover changes, too; Claudia and Gerry copied and enlarged old seed packets for the images.

The couple chose Wedgwood china from the hotel line; clear white and sturdy, it's produced in many shapes and sizes. Placement on the plate is part of the eye appeal of food, so Claudia loves "all the different shapes. Square plates, plates with rims, deep bowls—they all give inspiration to a pastry chef. I like to make up a dessert plate full of 'little tastes' that a diner can combine to please."

Claudia and Gerry met local farmers and vintners and found that "Our neighbors are eager to help. We wanted a menu that celebrated the very best of what was coming out of the ground seasonally, and we've found it." When the asparagus pops up, for example, Gerry produces spring garlic and white asparagus soup with Berkshire pancetta-wrapped roasted asparagus tips and Arbequina olive oil. And Claudia is as inventive, crafting a dessert plate that snaps up spring with a crostada with rhubarb jam and goat cheese cream.

PLATO

Award-winning designers Queensbury Hunt approached china design with fresh innovation, reflected in this 2006 set, *right*. Plates needn't be round, a square can encompass a circle, and all can be combined to add interest to the table. Mixing this geometry is the top note of their refined iconoclastic vision.

QUEENSWARE PLAIN

OPPOSITE AND BELOW RIGHT: The creamware known as Queensware for Queen Charlotte's patronage, has remained a favorite since its origin more than two centuries ago. This variation, Queensware Plain, is the simplest in design and finds favor with both modernists and traditionalists. It works as easily with silver and crystal as it does with less formal settings, and is known for its perfection as a backdrop for food.

SHAGREEN

BELOW LEFT: Wedgwood designers were inspired by the fine accoutrements of art deco. The use of shagreen—leather made from sharkskin—as a textured surface for small and elegant accessories was captured in this range.

JASPER CONRAN WHITE AND QUEENSWARE

The easy informality of this dining room in an Irish country house is a good backdrop to the generously proportioned Jasper Conran White. Long a contemporary designer, Conran cherishes the historic roots of Wedgwood and visited the archives as he worked on his new designs. In the country kitchen, with its long views over green turf and the sea, three Queensware bowls reflect the timelessness of this old design.

DRABWARE

In this boathouse by a river, *opposite,* cool shadows and quiet shades set the scene for a lunch on a sunny day. At the center of the scheme is a placesetting of drabware in the gentle khaki tones Josiah Wedgwood originated, reminiscent of sun-warmed stone. Old coin silver spoons, taupe linen napkins, a French quilt for a tablecloth, and a woven reed trunk for a serving table suggest that texture as well as color are important here.

On the table, *above left,* cream, tan, and taupe are the keys to keeping one's cool on a warm day; the candle is contained in a little basketweave votive, while a canvas bucket holds a bouquet of parrot tulips. Drabware first appeared in 1810.

The matchstick blinds temper the sunshine, and the simple shapes from the china to the chairs, *above right,* ensure a peaceful background to a quiet afternoon.

INDIA

In early spring daffodils spill streams of yellow to brighten a gray day in the English countryside. Bunches were gathered and arranged for a Sunday lunch in a Georgian room painted butter yellow. Designed in 1996, India was based on patterns and materials from the subcontinent. Designers at Wedgwood's Studio may study an original document, then abstract a few details; the creative department draws each design and experiments with color schemes and scale.

Among the shapes available is the classic globe, *above left,* a favorite at Wedgwood for many generations. These espresso cups are ready for the after-lunch linger.

Champagne, served in Wedgwood etched flutes garlanded with posies, *above,* is the starter to a long Sunday lunch.

The decoration on the dinner plate, *left,* is reduced to a frieze at the rim that echoes mosaics at the Taj Mahal, while the stylized flowers of the dessert plate are in gentle colors, as if mellowed with age.

OPPOSITE: An oval footed bowl of persimmons is inspired by the Chinese tiger motif in the Dynasty collection.

DYNASTY

Opulent, exotic Dynasty recalls the long influence Chinese design has had on the West. Historical references from earlier Wedgwood pieces were used for inspiration. As English traders packed their ships with tea and spices in the seventeenth century, they added porcelain, paintings, and furniture. Soon there was chinoiserie everywhere in England—a Chinese teahouse in the garden of an estate and teapots and teacups for the new beverage. As craftsmen took up the theme, every era had its interpretation, from Thomas Chippendale's use of fretwork to the Victorians' love of exotica—Chinese silk shawls, wallpaper, and porcelain—to the use of Chinese themes for room decoration in the twenties and thirties.

A vase in matte black with applied persimmon decoration shows the distinctive outline of the Chinese tiger at the top, as well as the Greek key.
Dynasty's wide choice of motifs and shapes allows any design element to be emphasized, whether a Greek key design, as on the saucers, or the large black and gilding charger.

ELLEN O'NEILL

Ellen O'Neill spends the workweek in a skyscraping apartment in New York City, where each night the Empire State Building sheds light on her aerie. On the weekends, however, she comes down to earth. Her own patch of earth, that is—two acres in the Hamptons countryside. In summer, she lets the field grow into a grass and wildflower meadow, then mows a path through it and sets a table at its center. "That's where I like to give my dinners, out under the sky and the stars." The breeze across the fields and the fragrance of sun-warmed greenery at the end of the day add to the pleasures to be found at the table.

"My weekend starts in the farmers' market," she says, and her weekend menu comes from that serendipity—as well as her table setting.

As an experienced designer who's worked in product development, interiors, and retailing, Ellen has a well-schooled eye. Her preferences at home are for the long-loved object that has a bit of a backstory and a clear palette of colors. Years of collecting mean she can have almost infinite possibilities for the table. "In this house," she says of her 1860s frame house with its turret, "I'm inclined to use red and white in decorating."

When she saw a shiny red metal table in the Paris flea market, of course it had to come home with her—it now is a cornerstone to her summer evenings. "I do like Chelsea Garden china from Wedgwood. It has a vintage feel, is as informal as I am, and those berries are red, which picks up the reds in my old linens." She'll pull out some of her vintage linens—in the red and white department alone she has toile, cottons, and paisley shawls among others to choose from, the easy mix adding its own refreshing twist to the pattern.

The view from the table is of the garden, so it's fitting that another aspect of the china Ellen likes is the garden-inspired design. "Sometimes it's the flowers that will help me set the table—when the lilacs are in bloom, I just gather armloads and take it from there."

On a warm afternoon, the shade of the terrace is a welcome retreat.

OPPOSITE, ABOVE: Jasper Conran's cups come in a variety of colors as mixed as a flower border and can be stacked to contrast or match.

OPPOSITE, BELOW: Looking fresh-picked, the berries and herbs on Chelsea Garden are botanically correct, perfect for lunch in the garden.

Once upon a time there were four little Rabbits, and their names were—Flopsy, Mopsy, Cotton-tail and Peter.

PETER RABBIT

At a cottage in Battersea a nursery tea for little friends is inspired by Beatrix Potter's Peter, as popular today as at his 1893 birth; these Wedgwood plates that tell of his adventures are a tradition for many families.

Beatrix Potter herself was happy to see her designs used in ways that delighted children; Wedgwood gained the right to use her drawings on china in 1949. Now many generations cherish this old childhood friend.

ABOVE LEFT: The menu is taken from the story—"Old Mrs. Rabbit took a basket and her umbrella. And went through the wood to the baker's. She bought a loaf of brown bread." Quail eggs, a tiny treat for small fingers, are to come.

BELOW LEFT: The magic of "once upon a time": A traditional present for a new baby, this set of plate, cup, and bowl is still a favorite among parents.

OPPOSITE, ABOVE LEFT: The egg cup cradles a hen's egg perfectly. The plate is the place for toast soldiers to be dipped carefully into the soft egg yolk.

OPPOSITE, ABOVE RIGHT: A set of mugs is just right for chamomile tea or cocoa; the bowls are perfect for soup or porridge.

OPPOSITE, BELOW LEFT: Chinaware for children was an important part of Wedgwood's line, especially during the nineteenth century.

OPPOSITE, BELOW RIGHT: Stacks of Peter Rabbit pottery await the next tea party and bring to life the watercolor illustrations that Beatrix Potter so lovingly rendered.

WILD STRAWBERRY

A table set with Wild Strawberry picks up the theme of a cream tea with strawberries; an antique creamware berry drainer serves the fruit, which is to be savored with scones and clotted cream. A row of potted strawberry plants edges the table.

Wild Strawberry is a perennially popular pattern. Van Day Truex, master of mid-twentieth-century design, was working at Tiffany when he saw original Wedgwood strawberry engravings from Josiah's time; he insisted that they were the perfect china pattern, if used in an overall strawberry design. He was proved right with his first order, which sold out immediately. "Good design is forever," he once said—as Wild Strawberry proves.

SWEET PLUM

One of Wedgwood's treasures is its voluminous archives that date back to founder Josiah's time. Each era adds its own favorites to the collection, and contemporary designers can find unlimited prompts to their creativity when they take some time to review the old design books. Wedgwood has long been known for its florals, and Sweet Plum is a translation of an old pattern reworked in size and design: It looks like the flowers have been liberated from antique chintz. Particularly popular in Japan, this gold-rimmed pattern can be used formally or in a casual setting.

FLORENTINE TURQUOISE

Any design historian knows that time and travel tend to layer elements of pattern in an unpredictable flow, with particular motifs appearing and reappearing in different places at different times. Just as Josiah Wedgwood adopted—and adapted—the works of the ancient potters, today we scan the discoveries of many cultures for inspiration. A piece like this bone china in the Florentine Turquoise pattern can be read like a history book. The sinuous pattern intertwines griffins and other animals, along with grotesque masks and interlaced arabesques, against the bold blue, as precious as old turquoise stones. This is a 1931 translation of a nineteenth-century original design, which in its turn spoke of the late Victorian revival of the gothic, and of their love of the exotic Eastern ends of the British Empire, evident in its complex Persian rug–like patterning.

CHATSWORTH

The delicate and rather formal pattern of Chatsworth china is the perfect choice for a dessert party. The side plates wait on a chest for guests to serve themselves a buffet of desserts. The Chatsworth setting contributes to the festive atmosphere, and each element draws interest, from the delicately painted rim to its embossed design that lends an added dimension to the arabesques of scrollwork.

APPLEY HOARE

When Appley Hoare opened her London antiques store with her daughter Zoe, it reflected their love of French furniture that was timeworn and cherished by generations. They scour the French countryside for furnishings with simple lines and well-rubbed paint. "We like them full of faded glory," says Zoe, who was brought up on the road, helping to hunt down treasures in French antiques markets.

Located at the Pimlico crossroads of London decorating chic, they offer a rich mix. "We like to sell what we love—customers who come to us want to know they are sharing our own tastes. There's an emotional element to this furniture—you remember how others lived, especially as most of it is in original condition, though a bit distressed," says Zoe. You might find a lichen-covered eighteenth-century stone bench, or a giant stone pig, or a cupboard in faded blue paint, or a pile of smart red-striped linen napkins to store inside it. "Visitors can't resist the urge to touch, whether the crisply ironed linens, or the rough old stone, or the tabletop smoothed by a hundred years of use," says Zoe.

The urge to mix and blend helped Zoe when she chose some Wedgwood tea sets that were designed for mixing together as you please, with coordinating prints and colors. With plenty of choices, visitors can have their pick by whim or mood. The Polka Dot pink cups have been added to the Harlequin collection, a new Wedgwood celebration of teatime.

"It's always teatime here. We put the kettle on and brew up some ginger tea, and fill a plate with organic biscuits," says Zoe as she settles in with a butterfly-handled teacup. One recent afternoon she and Appley brought in a cake from the bakery down the street, and were pleased to see how the pink icing set off the polka dots on one set of cups. "And we love flowers—we keep some blooming here always—and the butterfly-handled cups add just the right touch.

"Selling antiques is very sociable. When people come in for a browse, they like to talk about what's here and learn about its history. And, of course, those who buy come back again and again, and we really get to know each other," says Zoe, off to fill the biscuit plate again as another client begins to browse.

RIGHT: A traditional harlequin service contains pieces that vary but relate; it is either made that way or matched. "We sell chair sets, too, that are harlequin, with two or so styles that look good together," says Appley.

BELOW: Arranged on an old painted garden table, Polka Dot teacups with their thirties flair sit next to a cake with matching pink icing. Inspired by archive designs, the new pink Polka Dot service is a recent addition to others in turquoise and pale yellow and green. The backdrop is a collection of early French books bound in paper now mellowed with age.

LADY O'REILLY
THE FORMAL TABLE

Beyond the graceful Georgian windows, the gentle green folds of the Irish countryside stretch in all directions, in one of those long slow summer twilights that the country does so well. Inside the centuries-old walls of Castlemartin, the dining room is coming to life, as the candles are lit on the long mahogany table, the flames dancing in their reflection in the Waterford crystal chandelier overhead. Lady O'Reilly is entertaining tonight, and the table is laid with fine examples of the best Wedgwood, while the eighteenth-century pieces are on display around the room.

As the wife of the chairman of the board of Waterford Wedgwood, Lady O'Reilly would be expected to have a fine set or two of Wedgwood to use for their many dinners and receptions. But it was old Wedgwood that brought the couple together, and that still gives her pleasure, especially on nights like this, when the creamware sauceboats and baskets are in a setting like that for which they were made two hundred years ago: a fine Georgian room where the neoclassical nymphs on the white marble fireplace resemble those that decorated Josiah Wedgwood's jasper.

Greek in origin but raised in New York, Lady O'Reilly fell in love with antique Wedgwood years ago. "I collected majolica and creamware wherever I found it as I traveled, whether at flea markets or in fine antiques shops. After a few years I had a reasonable collection. I shared the interest with my brother."

In the mid-eighties, her family was interested in investing in the Wedgwood company, and her brother brought her along to a meeting as a Wedgwood enthusiast. There she met the investor Anthony O'Reilly, who was also interested in Wedgwood, which he merged with Waterford, two choice design houses with centuries of tradition.

The meeting of Chryss Goulandris and Sir Anthony O'Reilly eventually became a marriage, and now her

LEFT: In a regal Georgian house tucked away in Ireland's countryside, Sir Anthony and Lady O'Reilly set a formal dinner table. Always a Wedgwood collector, Lady O'Reilly, as the wife of the chairman of Waterford Wedgwood, has her favorites on the table, under the snowfall of crystal of a Waterford chandelier.

RIGHT: Lady O'Reilly mixes two of Wedgwood's most luxurious patterns, Tonquin and Black Astbury. Using the patterns in counterpoint adds to the lavish and luxurious effect, as does the gilding on jet black glaze. Candlelight brings its magic to an evening, with the Waterford Lismore glassware adding to the gleam. Roses from the garden are displayed simply in Waterford rose bowls, filling the air with scent.

OPPOSITE, ABOVE: For his seventieth birthday, Sir Anthony received the basalt epergne with its crystal baskets. A triumph of craftsmanship by the Wedgwood and Waterford artisans, the epergne was originally an eighteenth-century object that held sweetmeats for the end of the meal.

OPPOSITE, BELOW: Waterford crystal and antique silver set off the Black Astbury. The gilded decoration is raised to add a texture to the pattern.

collection of antiques has a place in the old house. The most precious pieces are in a corner cupboard, the back wall of which is painted green, a perfect backdrop to these delicate examples of the best Wedgwood. "I had done a lot of reading, and had helped when the Victoria and Albert did a show on Catherine the Great's Frog service. I was in a small antiques shop when I caught sight of a few pieces from her Husk service, which Josiah Wedgwood had made for her before the big commission for the Frog service. I was able to buy it all."

The Husk service is a premier example of Wedgwood at its finest, with a swag of pink around the plates, which were made in the simple and elegant Queen's shape. Josiah Wedgwood took the making of this service very seriously, saying he "trembled for the Russian service," and sending specialist painters to Chelsea for the decoration. Unlike the Frog service, which is on display in the Hermitage, some pieces of the Husk pattern do appear from time to time, and Lady O'Reilly was able to find them, each decorated with a flowing fuchsia flower

garland. "I love the creamware, especially the unusual pieces like the pair of vases and a cistern that I have."

With much of her time spent in philanthropy and the Castlemartin racing stud farm she runs, she finds the house is a wonderful place to entertain, its dining room a naturally festive space. She's picked the perfect Wedgwood for occasions small and great. "I loved a thirties pattern called Tonquin. We had it made in red and in black in small plates, so I could mix it in with the Black Astbury." Astbury is a luxurious pattern of deep black topped with a gilded flower pattern that requires twenty-one applications of gold to give it a raised effect—another element in the sparkle of the evening.

ABOVE: A pack of hounds at full gallop spiral around the bowl. This simple form dates to early Wedgwood and is a good backdrop to many designs.

OPPOSITE: Ready for Sunday lunch, the table is filled with conversation pieces, like the pie dish with the molded lettuce leaf finial.

MOIRA GAVIN
THE HUNT TABLE

As the CEO of Wedgwood, Moira Gavin knows a great deal about china. She also knows a great deal about the inside of airplanes and just what taxis look like around the world. Although she's based in London, her work takes her abroad almost constantly, which makes time at home even more precious. She drives to the Pennsylvania countryside as soon as she touches down back in the States, and a bit more than an hour later, she is home. "We love this house," she says. "I knew I wanted a big open kitchen where everyone could eat informally or just sit with a cup of tea." Important, too, were big windows and an open fire for the long winter, as well as shelves for her many china collections. Lots of shelves—she loves china, and is surrounded by temptation every day at work. "There are so many good antiques shops just down the road. And I do brake for tag sales."

She has always collected china. "I love it, all kinds, and I use it, too. But it's very decorative—that's why the open shelves are so appealing." The basement holds the backup pieces. "We have so many friends nearby, and I make the most of every minute I'm home," she says. "I love to set a big table and have everyone in for a Sunday lunch or supper by the fire."

Her shelves at home are filled with Wedgwood from many eras. She and her husband, Tom Bross, an enthusiastic horseman, chose Wedgwood's Hunting Scenes china with its rollicking huntsmen, designed in 1992. Some of what she owns, like the terra-cotta pie dish, are contemporary editions of designs from earlier times, while others are vintage. Also on the shelves, besides some of Moira's favorite chickens, is a sampling of two notable patterns.

Napoleon Ivy, on the third shelf, inspired by the exiled ruler's stay on Elba, was created in the 1950s. Although there are records of the British government's sending ivy-patterned Wedgwood wares to Napoleon, it was most likely a very different design: This large-leaf version is not seen in Wedgwood's eighteenth-century archives. It is still a much-loved example of Wedgwood earthenware.

"We designed the table, too," Moira explains. "It's a great frame for all the china—it makes the meal. And guests really enjoy talking about the china!"

LEFT: Stacks of hand-painted Napoleon Ivy, a popular motif in the 1950s.

ABOVE LEFT: Hunting Scenes china is simple in design, with a kick of humor, as the huntsmen gallop around the plate. Horn-handled cutlery keeps the flavor rustic.

ABOVE RIGHT: On the table is a handsome dish for game pie originally designed by Josiah Wedgwood; it was popular whenever the price of flour rose, making a pastry crust expensive.

HARMONY

The vocabulary of ornament is large, with much of it derived from the ancient originals. Certainly Josiah Wedgwood knew how to combine thousand-year-old motifs like olive leaves and acorns, goddesses and urns, and those classical details attracted the modern designers who pored over the eighteenth-century archives as they worked on Harmony. The collection shows how a new look at old favorites can lead to surprises, as well as added beauty. A garland, a basket of flowers, acanthus leaves, even a tiny goddess are inspired by eighteenth-century models but scaled differently, with more lyric beauty than academic rigor. Each plate size differs in pattern yet relates to the overall effect: a table set with blue and white china, a longtime favorite that looks to both the past and the present.

DISTINGUISHED
HOUSE OF WEDGWOOD
COLLECTION

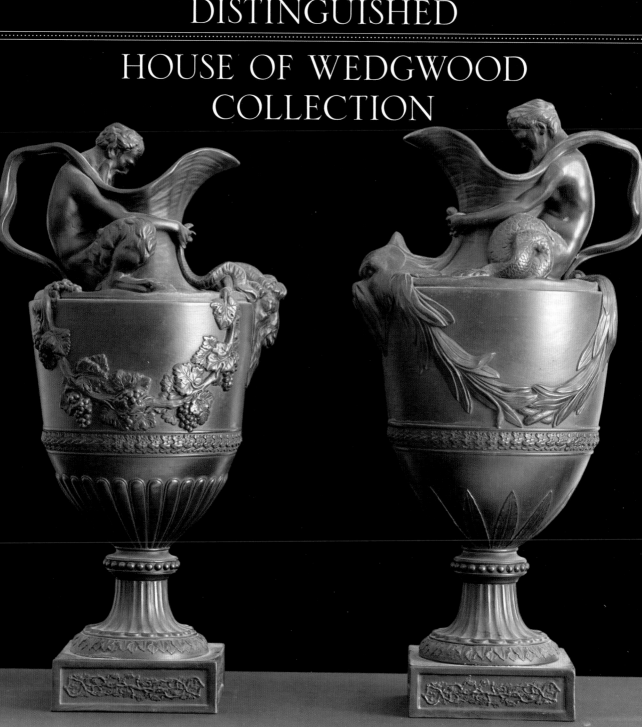

The most impressive products drawn from the heritage of Wedgwood design and craft are still available today in a special collection of pieces that demonstrates the skills—and the bravura—of these vases, bowls, and objets d'art. Most will be displayed as they were centuries ago—as the centerpiece of a table or as a prized object anyone would admire. Still crafted line for line, these are some of Wedgwood's best pieces originally from the 1700s and 1800s. They range from a Queensware orange bowl, which is a lyrical sphere of pierced china, to tall and formal examples of jasper that bring back the fine work of eighteenth-century designers and their white clay gods and goddesses, each cut out and applied, by hand, to black pieces of basalt with their burnished glow.

THE PRESTIGE COLLECTION

RIGHT: A black jasper bowl is ringed by the "dancing hours" originally designed by John Flaxman Jr. (1755–1826), a sculptor whom Josiah Wedgwood hired as he developed products to suit the neoclassical taste. The black basalt urn to its right, in its classically inspired perfection, recalls Josiah's overwhelming enthusiasm for the production of vases for display, sparking a Europe-wide "vase-mania."

BELOW: These creamware naiads with their net, produced in 1878, were originally intended as a fruit bowl or a table centerpiece.

OPPOSITE, ABOVE LEFT: A Queensware orange bowl was meant to display the golden orbs of the rare orange during the dessert course; the lid lifts off for serving. The latticework gave glimpses of the fruit inside and displayed the utmost in a potter's art. This design was illustrated in Wedgwood's first catalog of Queensware, in 1774.

OPPOSITE, ABOVE RIGHT: The simple elegance of black basalt is perfected in this bowl with its machined decoration. Named for the mineral basalt, which has been used since ancient times, Wedgwood's basalt can be polished and carved almost like stone itself.

OPPOSITE, BELOW LEFT AND RIGHT: More than a foot tall, these jasper candlelabra are eighteenth-century representations of the Roman goddesses Minerva and Diana. They were produced from 1782 and probably modeled by Flaxman.

RESOURCES

WEDGWOOD
www.wedgwood.co.uk
Wedgwood USA
www.wedgwoodusa.com

Auction Houses
Bonhams
www.bonhams.com

Christie's
www.christies.com

Skinner
www.skinnerinc.com

Sotheby's
www.sothebys.com

Antiques Shops
Appleby Antiques London
or
Stafford House, Stroud
0-777-828-2532
www.applebyantiques.net

Bardith
New York, NY
212-737-3775
www.bardith.com

The Country Dining Room
Great Barrington, MA
413-528-5050
www.countrydiningroomantiq.com

The Dining Room Shop
Barnes, London
0-208-878-1020
www.thediningroomshop.co.uk

Hollyhock
West Hollywood, CA
310-777-0100
www.hollyhockinc.com

Leo Kaplan Antiques
212-249-6766

Replacement Services
China Lane
888-737-5283
www.chinalane.com

China Search UK
0-192-651-2402
www.chinasearch.co.uk

Dishes from the Past
800-984-8801
www.dishesfromthepast.com

Replacements
888-737-5283
www.replacements.com

Set Your Table
800-600-2127
www.setyourtable.com

WEDGWOOD SOCIETIES
Wedgwood International Seminar
PO Box 674
Ontario, CA 91762-8674
www.w-i-s.org

Australia
Wedgwood Society of Australia
PO Box 190
Canterbury, Vic 3126

The Wedgwood Society of
New South Wales
www.users.bigpond.com/
thomaspz/wsnsw
SocietyNSW@gmail.com

The Wedgwood Society of
Queensland
PO Box 97
Annerley, QLD 4103

England
The Wedgwood Society
Friends of the Wedgwood Museum
www.wedgwoodmuseum.org.uk/
welcome.htm
june.bonell@wedgwoodmuseum
friends.org.uk

The Wedgwood Society of
Great Britain
www.geocities.com/Heartland/
3203/WSGB.html

United States
The Wedgwood Society of Boston
www.wedgwoodsociety.org

The Wedgwood Society of NY
www.wsny.org

The Wedgwood Society of
Southern California
www.wedgwoodsocal.org
info@wedgwoodsocal.org

The Wedgwood Society of
Washington, D.C.
www.wedgwoodcapital.org
WSofWDC@aol.com

MUSEUMS
England
The British Museum
London
www.britishmuseum.org

Liverpool Museum
Lady Lever Art Gallery
Wirral
www.liverpoolmuseums.org.uk/
ladylever/collections/
wedgwood.asp

Victoria and Albert
London
www.vam.ac.uk

The Wedgwood Museum Trust
Barlaston, Stoke-on-Trent
www.wedgwoodmuseum.org.uk

United States
Birmingham Museum of Art
Beeson Wedgwood Collection
Birmingham, AL
www.artsbma.org

Cooper-Hewitt
New York, NY
www.cooperhewitt.org

Metropolitan Museum of Art
New York, NY
www.metmuseum.org

Museum of Modern Art
New York, NY
www.moma.org

BIBLIOGRAPHY

Adams, Elizabeth Bryding. *The Dwight and Lucille Beeson Collection at the Birmingham Museum of Art.* Birmingham, Ala.: Birmingham Museum of Art, 1992.

Archer, S. M. *Josiah Wedgwood and the Potteries.* London: Longman, 1973.

Batkin, Maureen. *Wedgwood Ceramics 1846–1959: A New Appraisal.* London: Richard Dennis, 1982.

Bedford, John. *Wedgwood Jasperware.* New York: Walker, 1964.

Bindman, David. *John Flaxman.* London: Thames and Hudson, 1979.

Burton, Anthony. *Josiah Wedgwood: A Biography.* London: Andre Deutsch, 1976.

Buten, David. *18th Century Wedgwood: A Guide for Collectors and Connoisseurs.* New York and Methuen, Mass.: Main St. Press, 1980.

——. *Wedgwood and America: Wedgwood Bas-Relief Ware.* Merion, Pa.: Buten Museum, 1977.

Copeland, Robert. *Wedgwood Ware.* 2nd rev. ed. London: Shire, 2006.

Corkill, Margaret. *Wedgwood and His Ware.* Hertis, UK: Hatfield, 1973.

Dawson, Aileen. *Masterpieces of Wedgwood in the British Museum.* London: British Museum Press, 1984.

Dolan, Brian. *Josiah Wedgwood: Entrepreneur to the Enlightenment.* London: HarperCollins, 2004.

——. *Wedgwood: The First Tycoon.* New York: Viking, 2005.

Garrison, Gene. *Wedgwood.* Cincinnati, Ohio: Mosaic Press, 1982.

Gater, Sharon, and David Vincent. *The Factory in a Garden: Wedgwood from Etruria to Barlaston—the Transitional Years.* Staffordshire, UK: Keele Life Histories Centre, 1988.

Graham, John Meredith, and Hensleigh Wedgwood. *Wedgwood: A Living Tradition.* Brooklyn, N.Y.: Brooklyn Museum, 1948.

Herman, Michael. *Wedgwood Jasper: Classics, Rarities and Oddities from Four Centuries.* Atglen, Pa.: Schiffer, 2006.

——. *Wedgwood Jasperware: A Shape Book and Collector's Guide.* Atglen, Pa.: Schiffer, 2003.

Honey, W. B. *Wedgwood Ware.* London: Faber, 1948.

Keefe, Daniel J., III. *Wedgwood Ceramics.* Atglen, Pa.: Schiffer, 2005.

Kelly, Alison. *Decorative Wedgwood in Architecture and Furniture.* New York: Born-Hawes, 1965.

——. *The Story of Wedgwood.* London: Faber and Faber, 1962.

——. *Wedgwood Ware.* London and Sydney: Ward Lock, 1970.

Kemp, Ruth Vincent. *George Stubbs and the Wedgwood Connections.* Stoke-on-Trent, UK: Rushton and Turner, 1986.

Klamkin, Marian. *The Collector's Book of Wedgwood.* New York: Dodd Mead, 1971.

Koehn, Nancy F. *Brand New: How Entrepreneurs Earned Consumers' Trust from Wedgwood to Dell.* Boston: Harvard Business School Press, 2001.

Macht, Carol. *Classical Wedgwood Designs.* New York: Gramercy, 1957.

Mankowitz, Wolf. *The Portland Vase and the Wedgwood Copies.* London: Andre Deutsch, 1952.

Meteyard, Eliza. *The Wedgwood Handbook: A Manual for Collectors.* Ann Arbor, Mich.: Gryphon Books, 1971. Facsimile reprint of the 1875 edition.

Perry, Hamilton Darby. *Wedgwood Style: Three Centuries of Distinction.* New York: Freundlich Communications, 2001.

Rathbone, Frederick. *Old Wedgwood.* London: Bernard Quaritch, 1898; reprint, London 1968.

Reilly, Robin. *The Collector's Wedgwood.* Huntington, N.Y.: Portfolio Press, 1980.

——. *Josiah Wedgwood 1730–1795.* London: Macmillan, 1992.

——. *Wedgwood.* London: Macmillan, 1989.

——. *Wedgwood: The New Illustrated Dictionary.* Woodbridge, Suffolk, UK: Antique Collectors Club, 1995.

——. *Wedgwood Jasper.* London and New York: Thames and Hudson, 1994.

Tames, Richard. *Josiah Wedgwood.* London: Shire, 1987.

Towner, Donald. *Creamware.* London: Faber and Faber, 1978.

Uglow, Jenny. *The Lunar Men: The Friends Who Made the Future 1730–1810.* London: Faber and Faber, 2002.

Wedgwood, Barbara, and Hensleigh Cecil Wedgwood. *The Wedgwood Circle, 1730–1897: Four Generations of a Family and Their Friends.* Toronto: Collier Macmillan, 1980.

Wedgwood, Josiah C. *History of the Wedgwood Family,* 1908.

Williams, Peter. *Wedgwood: A Collectors Guide.* London: Quintet, 1992.

Young, Hilary. *The Genius of Wedgwood.* London: Victoria and Albert Museum, 1995.

GLOSSARY

BASALT WARE Wedgwood's black stoneware is a form of stoneware to which Josiah Wedgwood added manganese and iron oxide from local coal mines to stain the clay. Named for its resemblance to the mineral basalt, the lustrous black of this ware made it a fine choice for busts and cameos, as well as teapots and other tableware.

BONE CHINA Bone ash was added to a mix of china clay, flint, and feldspathic rock to produce bone china. Sturdy, light, translucent white chinaware, it was first perfected by Josiah Spode II at the end of the eighteenth century. Wedgwood's bone china was then improved upon by Josiah Wedgwood's son, John, and Josiah Wedgwood II, with the first pieces introduced in 1812. Lack of success in the market meant bone china was discontinued in 1831. The company returned to bone china production in 1878 with a perfected formula and designs and is still making bone china services.

CANEWARE An example of a vitreous body that is not porous. First cataloged by Wedgwood in 1787, caneware comes from clay that gives the finished pieces a fawn color. Tea sets shaped to resemble bamboo were a particular caneware favorite.

CREAMWARE Although creamware was made in Staffordshire before Josiah Wedgwood's time, he was determined to perfect its color and refine its glaze and body. His success in the production of an earthenware with a high percentage of a white clay and of shapes based on fine porcelain or silver tableware gave him a platform that he hadn't before had. Creamware was instantly popular and fashionable, and it was renamed Queensware when Queen Charlotte became a Wedgwood patron in 1765.

DRABWARE A stained and glazed earthenware originally perfected in 1810, and based on Queensware. Its distinctive khaki color either stood on its own or was a base for painted and printed decoration.

JASPERWARE One of the most popular and innovative of Josiah Wedgwood's creations, jasperware, an unglazed stoneware, is an adaptable material that has retained its popularity for more than two hundred years. It took many trials before it was perfected in 1777. The clay could be colored before being baked or later, with a slip, and the tints included several shades of blue, lavender, straw, green, lilac, gray, and brown. The fine colors were the perfect backdrop to apply white neo-classical figures inspired by Roman and Greek motifs.

PEARL WARE A white-bodied earthenware with a glaze to which cobalt oxide was added to increase the white effect. In 1779, after years of experimenting, Josiah Wedgwood named it *pearl* to emphasize its color, and used motifs painted in blue as a contrast. When the glaze pools, the blue tint can be seen.

STONEWARE Pottery of fusible rock and clay. Earliest examples are usually salt glazed, though later Wedgwood examples include white and colored stoneware called *porcelain* in the early nineteenth century.

WEDGWOOD BLUE A soft blue tone used on jasperware to contrast with the white of the applied classical figures. Another darker blue was also used, called Portland Blue, in reference to the famous Portland Vase.

WHITE WARE White earthenware that dates to 1805, a blend of flint, blue clay, china clay, and china stone. Fired at a very high temperature, then glazed in white, its superior strength made it useful for both utilitarian and decorative wares.

ACKNOWLEDGMENTS

Many thanks to all those who helped us bring this book of Wedgwood style together: Jeff McNamara, whose beautiful photographs bring the objects to life; Cathie Calvert, whose love of Wedgwood and infatuation with Josiah told us their stories; Marysarah Quinn whose design meshed the old and new in the perfect way; Doris Cooper, whose personal passion for Wedgwood enabled us to do this book; Deborah Geltman, who kept us going with her wisdom and enthusiasm; and Lauren Shakely, for her continued support over the years. And thanks to all those at Clarkson Potter for their efforts in keeping our book on track: Kate Tyler, Andrew Stanley, Mark McCauslin, Donna Passannante, Derek Gullino, and Angelin Borsics. And to our assistants, Marlene Hand, our on-the-scene tech support; and Danielle Schiffman, for all her wonderful research.

Along the way, we discovered new friends who loved to show us their Wedgwood. They invited us into their homes to share their collections and set beautiful tables, each in their own personal style. I hope you'll enjoy all their stories in these pages: Carolyne Roehm, Thomas O'Brien, Charlotte Moss, Christine Maly, Roy Hardin, Moira Gavin, Ellen O'Neill, Stephen Drucker, Diane and Bob Martinson, Suzanne Rheinstein, Michael Smith, James Huniford, Sylvia Weinstock, Claudia Fleming and Gerry Hayden, Steve Wolf , Barbara Barry, Vera Wang, Martha Stewart, and Jasper Conran.

I also want to thank friends in England and Ireland for their warm welcome, taking such good care of me and Jeff on our travels and having cups of tea at the ready: Zoe and Appley Hoare, whose style has always been an inspiration; Sarah Calendar and Peter Beckett of Combermere Abbey, whose beautiful setting provided the backdrop for our prestige collections; Susie and Denis Tinsley, for always being up for our photo shoots and making us feel so at home with them; Katrin Cargill, who helped us with our locations and cheered us on; and Tom Carpenter, our host at Jane Austen's house. Many thanks also to John Pawson for letting us include his entertaining style and design philosophy in our pages.

My special appreciation goes to friends at Wedgwood for their support and personal love of Wedgwood: Lady O'Reilly, Moira Gavin, and Lord Wedgwood; and to those who lent a hand behind the scenes at Wedgwood in making this book happen: Julie Bukalders, Carole Hammersley, Michael Craig, Michelle Richards, Lester Gribetz, and Patty Yenesal.

93

94

97

99